TEENS ~ RELATIONSHIPS
WITH PEOPLE, PLACES AND THINGS

Facilitator Reproducible
Activities for Groups
and Individuals

Ester R.A. Leutenberg
Carol Butler, MS Ed, RN, C

Illustrated by
Amy L. Brodsky, LISW-S

publisher of therapy, counseling, and self-help resources

Whole Person Associates
101 West 2nd Street, Suite 203
Duluth, MN 55802

800-247-6789

Books@WholePerson.com
WholePerson.com

Teens – Relationships with People. Places and Things
Facilitator Reproducible Activities for Groups and Individuals

Copyright ©2014 by Ester R.A. Leutenberg and Carol Butler. All rights reserved. Except for short excerpts for review purposes and materials in the activities and handouts sections, no part of this book may be reproduced or transmitted in
any form by any means, electronic or mechanical without permission in writing from the publisher. Activities and handouts are meant to be photocopied.

All efforts have been made to ensure accuracy of the information contained in this book as of the date published. The author(s) and the publisher expressly disclaim responsibility for any adverse effects arising from the use or application of the information contained herein.

Printed in the United States of America

Editorial Director: Carlene Sippola
Art Director: Joy Morgan Dey

Library of Congress Control Number: 2014909593
ISBN: 978-157025-318-8

Introduction

Purpose of the Book

Teens usually connect the word *relationships* with other people. *Teens ~ Relationships with People, Places and Things* broadens the scope of relationships:

Places – home, school, cyberspace, situations likely to have a positive or negative influence on teens, resources to meet their needs and *mental destinations*.

Things – technology, money, possessions, career considerations, and potentially addictive substances and activities.

as well as ...

People – those closest to teens during their formative years, plus their relationship with **Self**: their mind's eye image, self-efficacy versus self-sabotage, thought-driven feelings, external and internal messages, the power of words, *esteem-able* actions, mental and physical health.

This workbook covers the following teen connections:

1. **Family/People at Home** – primary experiences that affect teens' views of how people live their lives.
2. **Peers** – possibly the most influential people during adolescence.
3. **Romantic Partners** – first love that awakens and intensifies emotions.
4. **Places** – physical locations, the memories and impact.
5. **Tangible Things** – money and materialism, and their degree of importance in teens' lives.
6. **Intangible Things** – ideas, traits and influences that contribute to character.
7. **Self** – a powerful relationship that affects all other alliances.

The activities in this workbook address real life relationships.

Ideally, teens ...

- Express thoughts and feelings, and gain insight.
- Share handouts at home which initiates communication.
- Engage in group activities and connect with peers.
- Share their work and build trust.
- Listen to disclosures and develop empathy.
- Discuss and debate, and develop open-mindedness.
- Recognize romantic issues and then choose caring partners.
- Identify powerful places, and appreciate and seek productive environments.
- Modify their place of mind and find peace of mind
- Prioritize possessions and evaluate their worth.
- Articulate intangibles and bring out and/or develop positive qualities.

TEENS – Relationships with People, Places and Things

Format of the Book

Introduction for Teen Participants motivates teens for the activities (page vi) and can be distributed prior to the first session to prepare teens for participation.

Cover Page for each chapter provides a quotation that can be used as an introduction to the chapter, and a brief description of each session, to assist facilitators in selecting topics. The cover page may be given to teens to interest them in upcoming activities.

Seven Chapters, four to eleven sessions per chapter.

Activities – A selection provides flexibility for the facilitator to choose those activities that meet participants' needs on various occasions. A timely topic may warrant a workshop, a series of sessions, or "stand alone" sessions. Facilitators are urged to "skip around" to find a format and subject that fits the situation for particular groups' or individuals' needs. Handouts can be used for individual introspection, interaction, artistic expression, games, music, poetry, drama, etc.

1. **My Relationships with Family / People at Home**
   Ways to deal with secrets, conflict, control, etc., and how to build love, resilience and trust; how teens wish to be treated and their treatment of caregivers; skills to stop power struggles, ways to problem solve and compromise; develop insight into dynamics in many types of families: bonds that link, in whom to confide, forgiveness, etc.

2. **My Relationships with Peers**
   Ways to minimize jealousy and enmeshment, expand social supports and strengthen personal development; fear of missing out; cliques; embarrassment; cookie cutter categorizations; inclusion, possible motives of people who exclude; invisible scars left by cruelty; ways to *leave marks* of hope and healing, etc.

3. **My Relationships with Romantic Partners**
   Healthy and unhealthy romance, ways to recognize and stop dating violence and other abuse, relationship costs and benefits; ways to emerge stronger and wiser after a break up, respectfully initiate a break up, argue agreeably, understand jealousy, decide what love is and isn't; amusement ride analogies, etc.

4. **My Relationships with Places**
   Positive and/or negative effects of one's most memorable home; places likely to foster optimal development or have detrimental effects; how attitudes toward school affect experiences; ways to work on solutions and not dwell on problems; explore how one's *place* of mind affects one's *peace* of mind, etc.

5. **My Relationships with Tangible Things**
   Technology's social, emotional, educational and other uses and abuses; explore how money talks (or NOT); identify prized possessions, think about whether one owns or is owned by belongings; materialism; define objects with little monetary value but significant meaning, etc.

6. **My Relationships with Intangible Things**
   Ways to make the most of time and life, freedoms and responsibilities; when to conform or not; pros and cons of competition and cooperation; the magnitude of small acts of kindness, compassion's benefits to others and oneself; beliefs; little things that are big, things that are broken, silent things that are loud, etc.

7. **My Relationship with Myself**
   Learn about self-image and actualization; define ways to support not sabotage oneself; learn how thoughts affect feelings, how to filter out destructive thoughts and consider constructive criticism; acknowledge ways words can hurt or heal; define value of esteem-able actions; mental and physical health, etc.

In each session

- **Reproducible handout(s) for participants:** photocopy one copy for each participant.
- **Changes to reproducible handout:** white out or add text to your photocopy and reproduce.
- *For the Facilitator* **(found on the back of each handout) provides the following:**
  I. Purpose: Goals for the teens.
  II. General Comments: Brief background information.
  III. Possible Activities: Ideas to introduce and present topics with answer keys or responses to elicit.
  IV. Enrichment Activities: Additional learning opportunities, ways to close session and/or follow up.

Introduction

Suggestions for Facilitators

Prepare quickly and easily – read handout(s) and facilitator information; decide which option to use if individual, team, or other formats are described; photocopy; follow directions to cut on broken lines, etc.

Teen and Facilitator Pages

Encourage introspection through
- Amusement park analogies
- Illustrations, diagrams, graphs, continuums and an alphabet acrostic
- Lists, sentence completions, fill in the blanks, matching exercises
- Posters, drawings, cartoons, collages, icons
- Quotations to analyze and personalize
- Scenarios in which teens decide what to do
- Self assessments
- Texts, blogs, poems, slogans
- Thought bubbles, visualization

Promote interaction through
- Brainstorming and board activities
- Discussion, debate, speeches
- Random acts of kindness for peers whose name is drawn, altruistic actions elsewhere
- Skits, role plays, pantomimes
- Teamwork, panel discussions
- Word and letter clue games, BINGO, quiz shows

Suggestions

Minimize mechanics – tell teens that unedited expression matters more than spelling or artistic ability.

Present one session from each chapter at subsequent meetings, to cover people, places, tangible and intangible things in a brief span of time, then present a second session from each chapter, etc. Varied interests and needs will be addressed, rather than several sessions on only one aspect of relationships.

Each chapter or a series of sessions may be a workshop.

Each session may stand alone.

Most sessions are adaptable for individual or group activities; allow at least fifty minutes for each session.

Confidentiality – remind teens:
What happens in group stays in group.
Disclose within one's comfort zone; no one is pushed to participate.
Use name codes, not actual names. (Ex: if a partner was abusive, use PWA for "partner was abusive.")

Exceptions to confidentiality – tell teens:
Some secrets are dangerous – if a teen discloses to a peer thoughts about harm to self, others, abuse, addiction or other serious issue, accompany the person as they tell a trusted adult, go to a hospital emergency department or call 911 or their local emergency services number.
If necessary, break confidentiality to save a life.

Encourage teens to talk privately after session if overwhelming emotions or issues surface; remind them that professional help and support groups are available.

Refer troubled teens for a professional evaluation if danger to self, others, abuse, addiction or other serious issues are suspected; call 911 or the local emergency services if danger is imminent.

Our gratitude to the following for their exceptional input –

Beth Jennings, CTEC Counselor
Hannah Lavoie, Teenage Consultant
Art Director – Joy Dey
Editorial Director – Carlene Sippola
Editor and Lifelong Teacher – Eileen Regen
Illustrator Amy L. Brodsky
Proofreader – Jay Leutenberg

Introduction for Teen Participants

> *"Tug on anything at all and you'll find it connected to everything else in the universe."*
> ~ John Muir

Think about your connections ...

You live with **you** 24/7.
You are linked with **family** or other people.
You are surrounded with **peers** at school.
You value **friends**.
You have, or may have in the future, **romantic partners**.
You enter **cyberspace**.
You experience physical **places**.
Your have **money** and **possessions**.
You could be affected by **addictions**.
You will pursue a **career**.
You are connected to your **intangibles**:

- Beliefs
- Competitive tendencies
- Conformity and non-conformity
- Cooperative efforts
- Decisions
- Emotions
- Freedoms
- Ideas
- Time
- Other traits

Through the activities you will "tug on" the people, places and things in your life and ...

Learn about and like yourself.
Grow in any type of family.
Deal with peer issues.
Shape your friendships.
Handle having, losing, or leaving a partner.
Position yourself where you will thrive.
Place your mind where you will find peace.
Determine the worth of the material things that matter to you.
Visualize the person you want to be
Tune in to what your heart feels is driving you.
Contribute to your character.
Create opportunities to show you care.

You will improve your connections "to everything else in the universe."

Introduction

Teens – Relationships with People, Places and Things

TABLE OF CONTENTS

1. My Relationships with Family/People at Home 11

    Ways I Wish to be Treated 13
        Ways I Wish to be Treated for the Facilitator 14
    Tug-of-War 15
        Tug-of-War for the Facilitator 16
    Family Feuds 17
        Family Feuds for the Facilitator 18
    Bonds that Link 19
        Bonds that Link for the Facilitator 20
    Tell and Trust 21
        Tell and Trust for the Facilitator 22
    Fridge Magnet Forgiveness 23
        Fridge Magnet Forgiveness for the Facilitator 24
    Fam-Lingo BINGO 25
        Fam-Lingo BINGO for the Facilitator 26

2. My Relationships with Peers 27

    Shape-ing Friendships 29
        Shape-ing Friendships for the Facilitator 30
    Friends and Cliques 31
        Friends and Cliques for the Facilitator 32
    Quote Apps 33
        Quote Apps for the Facilitator 34
    Afraid of Missing Out? 35
        Afraid of Missing Out? for the Facilitator 36
    Inclusion Pantomimes 37
        Inclusion Pantomimes for the Facilitator 38
    Play Ball? 39
        Play Ball? for the Facilitator 40
    Embarrassment Happens – I Embarrassed Myself 41
    Embarrassment Happens – I Embarrassed Someone 42
    Embarrassment Happens – Someone Embarrassed Me 43
        Embarrassment Happens for the Facilitator 44
    Cookie Cutter Categories 45
        Cookie Cutter Categories for the Facilitator 46
    The Marks Humans Leave 47
        The Marks Human Leave for the Facilitator 48

3. My Relationships with Romantic Partners ... 49

- Loves Me, Loves Me Not ... 51
  - Loves Me, Loves Me Not for the Facilitator ... 52
- BitterSweet Dating Violence ... 53
  - BitterSweet Dating Violence for the Facilitator ... 54
- Costs and Benefits ... 55
  - Costs and Benefits for the Facilitator ... 56
- Amusement Park Analogies ... 57
  - Amusement Park Analogies for the Facilitator ... 58
- Does Break Up = Broken Heart? ... 59
  - Does Break Up = Broken Heart? for the Facilitator ... 60
- Leave Respectfully ... 61
  - Leave Respectfully for the Facilitator ... 62
- Romantic Jealousy: The Other Side of the Coin ... 63
  - Romantic Jealousy: The Other Side of the Coin for the Facilitator ... 64
- Argue Agreeably ... 65
  - Argue Agreeable for the Facilitator ... 66
- What Love Is and What Love Is Not ... 67
  - What Love Is and What Love Is Not for the Facilitator ... 68

4. My Relationships with Places ... 69

- My Most Memorable Childhood Home ... 71
  - My Most Memorable Childhood Home for the Facilitator ... 72
- Location, Location, Location ... 73
  - Location, Location, Location for the Facilitator ... 74
- People at My School ... 75
  - People at My School for the Facilitator ... 76
- Place of Mind ... 77
  - Place of Mind for the Facilitator ... 78

5. My Relationships with Tangible Things ... 79

- My Techno-Logic ... 81
  - My Techno-Logic for the Facilitator ... 82
- $$$ Talks (or NOT) ... 83
  - $$$ Talks (or NOT) for the Facilitator ... 84
- My Most Prized Possessions ... 85
  - My Most Prized Possession for the Facilitator ... 86
- Slices of a Career Pie ... 87
  - Slices of a Career Pie for the Facilitator ... 88
- What Gets the Best of Me? My Robbers ... 89
- What Gets the Best of Me? My Susceptibilities ... 90

What Gets the Best of Me? My Best That it Gets	91
What Gets the Best of Me? for the Facilitator	92

6. My Relationships with Intangible Things 93

Your Time Is …	95
Your Time Is … for the Facilitator	96
Fortune Cookie Freedom	97
Fortune Cookie Freedom for the Facilitator	98
Go With the Flow?	99
Go With the Flow? for the Facilitator	100
Expanding Ideas to Contribute to My Character - I Believe …	101
Expanding Ideas to Contribute to My Character - Little Things that are Big	102
Expanding Ideas to Contribute to My Character - Things that are Broken	103
Expanding Ideas to Contribute to My Character - Silent Things that are Loud	104
Expanding Ideas to Contribute to My Character - Things I Would Not Want to Lose	105
Expanding Ideas to Contribute to My Character for the Facilitator	106
Rivalry Rhymes	107
Rivalry Rhymes for the Facilitator	108
Great Moments	109
Great Moments for the Facilitator	110
Ripples of Kindness	111
Ripples of Kindness for the Facilitator	112

7. My Relationship with Myself 113

Am I My Worst Enemy or Best Friend?	115
Am I My Worst Enemy or Best Friend? for the Facilitator	116
My Feelings	117
My Feelings for the Facilitator	118
In One Ear and …	119
In One Ear and … for the Facilitator	120
The Power of Words	121
The Power of Words for the Facilitator	122
Esteem-able	123
Esteem-able for the Facilitator	124
Passwords for My Health	125
Passwords for My Health for the Facilitator	126
What You See …	127
What You See … for the Facilitator	128
Are you Centered?	129
Are You Centered? for the Facilitator	130

MY RELATIONSHIPS WITH FAMILY/PEOPLE AT HOME ❶

I know why families were created with all their imperfections. They humanize you. They are made to make you forget yourself occasionally, so that the beautiful balance of life is not destroyed.

~ ANAIS NIN

Ways I Wish to Be Treated .... page 13 ▶
Teens compare how they wish parents/caregivers would treat them to how they actually are treated. Teens consider the benefits of treating caregivers as teens want to be treated and to warrant privileges.

Tug-of-War .... page 15 ▶
Teens identify and are helped to find ways to stop power struggles as they work toward independence. Teens consider problem solving and compromising, and determine when to drop the rope.

FAMILY FEUDS .... page 17 ▶
Teens explore dynamics in all types of families; how members compete and pull in opposite directions. Teens share their reactions to parental separation, stepfamily challenges, foster or group home placement.

Bonds That Link .... page 19 ▶
Teens recognize bonds beyond biological relatives, which link family members or people who live together. Teens discover better ways to bond through communication, and have mutual respect and joy in each other's life.

Tell and Trust .... page 21 ▶
Teens identify trusted adults in whom they can confide as well as the possibility of a friend breaching their trust. Teens analyze a quote that compares lies and secrets to a "cancer in the soul."

Fridge Magnet Forgiveness .... page 23 ▶
Teens receive lines from short poems about forgiveness to put into rhyming order. Teens compose their own refrigerator magnet messages about family forgiveness.

Fam-Lingo Bingo .... page 25 ▶
Teens express ideas about issues, attitudes and behaviors towards families. Teens discuss safety, secrets, addiction, conflict, control, emotional intimacy, resilience, respect, trust, etc.

My Relationships with Family/People at Home ▶

Ways I Wish to Be Treated

I Wish My Caregiver Would…	How My Caregiver Treats Me	How I Treat My Caregiver
Love me no matter what.		
Realize that I am almost an adult.		
Spend more time with me.		
Encourage me.		
Listen to me.		
Accept the way I feel.		
Respect that I have the right to my own opinions.		
Trust me.		
Care about my health without nagging me.		
Care about my safety without overprotecting me.		
Give me feedback in a constructive way.		
Accept that my best is good enough.		
Allow me to pursue my own school and career goals.		
Make rules appropriate to my maturity level.		
Get to know my friends before forming opinions.		

TEENS – Relationships with People, Places and Things

Ways I Wish to Be Treated
FOR THE FACILITATOR

I. Purpose
To treat parents/caregivers as teens wish to be treated.

II. General Comments
Teens will realize that they often treat parents in the same way that they resent the manner in which their parents treat them.

III. Possible Activities
   a. Ask teens how they want to be treated by parents/caregivers (like young adults not kids, etc.).
   b. Distribute the *Ways I Wish to Be Treated* handout and ask for a few examples.
   c. Write examples on the board as teens dictate ideas.

   Possibilities

I Wish My Caregiver Would…	How My Caregiver Treats Me	How I Treat My Caregiver
Love me no matter what.	*Ex:* They love me when I obey.	*Ex:* Love them even when they say "No."
Respect that I have the right to my own opinions.	*Ex:* Sometimes they talk down to me.	*Ex:* Sometimes I talk disrespectfully to them.

   d. Emphasize that there are no right or wrong answers; responses will be based on individual experiences.
   e. Allow time for completion.
   f. Encourage teens to share their responses and receive peer feedback.
   g. Emphasize that teens can:
      - Treat parents/caregivers as teens want to be treated.
      - Warrant privileges by acting responsibly.

IV. Enrichment Activities
   - Write *I wish my teen would …* on the board.
   - Ask teens to brainstorm their parent/caregivers' wish lists.
   - Recruit a volunteer to list the group's ideas on the board.
   - Encourage teens to identify which wishes are reasonable.
   - Ask participants to identify which wishes benefit the teens.
   - Encourage teens to brainstorm:
      – Ways teens can change, or make the situation better.
      – Ways the caregivers can change, or make the situation better.

Tug-of-War

A tug-of-war is a struggle to win with both sides pulling at opposite ends of the rope.

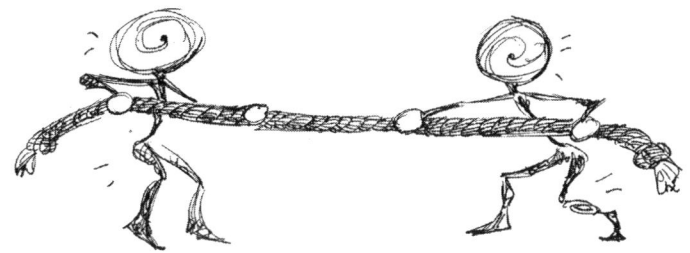

1. In what situation do you and your parent / caregiver _____ get into a tug-of-war?
   _{NAME CODE}
   _____
   _____

2. Place an "X" on your location on the continuums below.

   The **issue** matters most.   My **power** matters most.
   _____

   This person **cares about me**.   This person **does not care about me**.
   _____

   I **trust** this person.   I **distrust** this person.
   _____

3. If more "X's" are **closer to the left side** of this page, how can you **compromise**?
   _____
   _____

4. If more "X's" are **closer to the right side** of this page, how can you stop the **power struggle**?
   _____
   _____

5. Are you possibly **pulling against** someone who is **pulling for you**?
   _____
   _____

6. Explain. _____
   _____
   _____
   _____

TEENS – Relationships with People, Places and Things

Tug-of-War
FOR THE FACILITATOR

I. Purpose
To identify and stop power struggles.

II. General Comments
Teens may struggle against parents/caregivers to gain a greater sense of self, strength and independence.

Teens need help to recognize when a trusted and caring person is trying to assist them.

III. Possible Activities
   a. Before session coach two volunteers to pull on opposite ends of a notebook.
   b. At the start of session volunteers portray a tug-of-war with the notebook.
   c. Ask group members to guess what is going on (tug-of-war).
   d. Write *Power Struggle* on the board.
   e. Ask how it relates to tug-of-war (people try to grab control).
   f. Distribute the *Tug-of-War* handout and allow time for completion.
   g. Encourage teens to share responses and receive peer feedback.
   h. Encourage a discussion about ways to compromise.
   i. **Possibilities:**
      - Share views.
      - Both people listen.
      - Brainstorm options.
      - Agree on mutually acceptable solutions.
   j. Encourage a discussion about ways to stop power struggles.
      Possibilities:
      - Work to solve the problem rather than to win.
      - Realize you probably will not gain power over the person.
      - Gain power over yourself through positive thoughts and actions.
      - Be respectful even if you think it's undeserved.
      - Ask a trusted adult for help to deal with the issue.
      - Seek counseling if you experience abuse, anger, depression, etc.
   k. Write *When is it time to drop the rope?* on the board.
   l. Ask teens to brainstorm responses; a volunteer lists their ideas.
      Possibilities:
      - When both people relentlessly pull harder and harder against each other.
      - When the issue isn't worth it.
      - When the relationship means more than to have your own way.
      - When letting go will give you peace.
      - When continuing will cause you harm.
      - When your needs can be met another way.

IV. Enrichment Activities
   a. Write on the board and ask teens to discuss:
      - *Don't push and pull to get your way, appeal to the person's generosity.* (Persuasively ask for what you want; the person may grant it).
   b. Write on the board and ask teens to discuss:
      - *Sometimes the bigger person backs down.* (Recognize when someone is unwilling to negotiate; find another way to stick to your beliefs).

My Relationships with Family/People at Home ▶

FAMILY FEUDS

1. Check the boxes in front of all of the people with whom you live.

    ❏ Adoptive parent   ❏ Foster parent   ❏ Half sibling

    ❏ Adoptive sibling   ❏ Foster sibling   ❏ Step parent

    ❏ Biological parent   ❏ Group home caregiver   ❏ Step sibling

    ❏ Biological sibling

    ❏ Adoptive, bio, foster, group, half or step, grandparent or other adult relative

    ❏ Adoptive, bio, foster, group, half or step, partner or housemate

    ❏ Other _____

2. In your family, who *pulls* at whom?

    _____
    _____
    _____

3. How do your family members *pull* in opposite directions?

    _____
    _____
    _____

4. In what ways are you affected?

    _____
    _____
    _____

5. How can you avoid being pulled?

    _____
    _____
    _____

6. Who is a trusted adult who can help you? Why have you listed this person?

    _____
    _____
    _____

TEENS – Relationships with People, Places and Things

FAMILY FEUDS
FOR THE FACILITATOR

I. Purpose
To identify how family members compete and teens get pulled apart; to formulate possible solutions.

II. General Comments
Teens explore some of the dynamics in different types of families.

III. Possible Activities
   a. Before session ask for three volunteers to portray two people (gently) pulling a middle person in opposite directions.
   b. At the start of session the volunteers perform; elicit what is happening from the audience.
   c. After actors are seated, ask teens to share times they felt pulled in two different directions.
   d. Distribute the *Family Feuds* handout and allow time for completion.
   e. Reinforce confidentiality: "What is said in this room stays in this room."
   f. Ask for a show of hands regarding who checked specific boxes at the top of the page.
   g. Allow teens to look around to see people with similar family types.
   h. Encourage teens to share their responses (within their comfort zones) and receive peer feedback.
      Examples
      1. Addressed by the show of hands. (see f. above)
      2. A parent may be torn between their teen and their spouse or partner.
      3. Members compete for attention, affection, time, energy, money, equal treatment.
      4. A teen may be in the middle with parents pulling in opposite directions after a break up.
      5. Discuss rights, responsibilities, rules, roles and privileges especially in new situations.
      6. Open communication, compromise, reassurance regarding love, family counseling if needed.
   i. Emphasize that regardless of current family type, knowledge of others will help teens gain empathy.
   j. Explain that in adulthood teens may be in step, foster or adoptive families or discover half siblings.
   k. Encourage a discussion about step families: it's normal to feel intruded upon by a new step parent and step siblings; it's helpful to spend some time alone with your biological parent as well as doing activities with the whole family; do not be the messenger or mediator between separated parents; a step parent does not replace a parent; it is not disloyal to a biological parent to bond with a step parent; a change in status as an only child or the oldest or youngest may seem strange; jealousy and other dynamics are understandable and may subside; the *step-situation* is a challenge for all but rewards can be a larger support system, exposure to different cultures, and adaptability.
   l. Promote an exploration of foster families and group homes: it's normal to feel guilty or stigmatized about family problems but it is not their fault; feelings of grief, loss and love despite abuse are common; fear about a new home and strangers as caregivers will eventually subside; biological siblings that stay together are buffers against adversity and help each other's resilience; it is tough to enter a new school and try to make new friends but it can be done; use sources of support – social workers, school counselors, extracurricular activities, spirituality; know that reunification into a healthier family may occur if parents receive treatment for addiction, parenting skills, financial and social support, etc.
   m. Initiate a discussion about adoptive families: it's not disloyal to adoptive parents to wonder about birth parents, what they look like, why they gave up a child, what their personality traits, talents and interests are, and about their health histories; teens may fear they inherited addiction or other potentially harmful trait but need to know that environment and personal choices about lifestyle are powerful factors.

IV. Enrichment Activities
Encourage discussion about teens who are angry at biological families for giving them up; elicit that possibly their parents chose to give them a better life.

My Relationships with Family / People at Home ▶

Bonds That Link

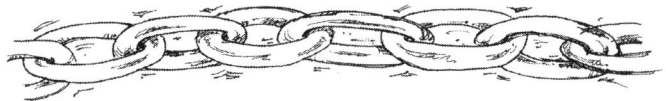

Birth Parents   Birth Children   Full/Half Siblings

Adoptive Parents   Adoptive Children   Adoptive Siblings

Step Parents   Step Children   Step Siblings

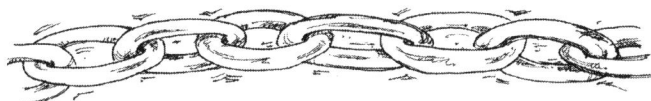

Foster Parents   Foster Children   Foster Siblings

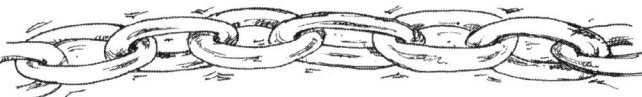

Group Home Caregivers Group Home Children   Group Home Peers

I think the bonds that link ALL of the above are ...

1. _____
2. _____
3. _____
4. _____
5. _____

I can better bond with members of my family by . . .

TEENS – Relationships with People, Places and Things

Bonds That Link
FOR THE FACILITATOR

I. **Purpose**
   To illustrate bonds, beyond biological relatives, that link family members or teens in other settings with their caregivers and peers; to portray these connections.

II. **General Comments**
   Conflict can often be quelled by considering connections among people living together.

III. **Possible Activities**
   a. Before session label 15 sheets of paper with a thick marker (*Biological Parents, Biological Children, Full/Half Siblings, Adoptive Parents, Adoptive Children, Adoptive Siblings, Step Parents, Step Children, Step Siblings, Foster Parents, Foster Children, Foster Siblings, Group Home Caregivers, Group Home Children* and *Group Home Peers*).
   b. Tape a sign on each of 15 volunteers; they stand in the front of the room and hold hands. Alternatively tape the papers together in a chain and stick them to the board.
   c. Ask the group:
      "What do these people have in common?" (members of a family or community, etc.)
      "What do they NOT have in common?" (not all are blood relatives).
   d. Volunteers remove their signs and return to their seats.
   e. Distribute the *Bonds that Link* handout.
   f. Allow time for completion.
   g. Encourage teens to share their responses and receive peer feedback.
      Possibilities
      I think bonds that link ALL of the above are …
      - Appreciation
      - Caring
      - Commitment
      - Common problems
      - Communication
      - Dislike of same person
      - Dissatisfied with home life
      - Flexibility
      - Forgiveness
      - Joy
      - Like talents and/or interests
      - Love
      - Respect
      - Same bad habits or issues
      - Spirituality
      - Teamwork
      - Other _____
      - Other _____

      I can better bond with members of my *family* by … (focusing on their positive qualities, etc.).
   h. Write this quotation on the board. Prompt teens to agree or disagree and apply it to their families.

   The bond that links your true family is not one of blood,
   but of respect and joy in each other's life.
   ~ Richard Bach

IV. **Enrichment Activities**
   a. Distribute plain or colored paper and ask teens to cut into strips; supply markers and tape.
   b. Ask teens to write their bonds that help link families together on the strips with color magic markers, then tape strips together in a long paper chain. If allowed, photograph and post the picture of the group wrapped in the chain of positive words.
   c. Encourage discussion and debate about issues related to different types of families.
      Possibilities
      - Is it better for the biological parent to discipline teens or for the stepparent and birth parent to work together? Explain.
      - If you are or were adopted, would you want to meet your birth parents? Explain.
      - If you are or were in foster care, what would be your greatest fear? Explain.

My Relationships with Family/People at Home ▶

Tell and Trust
INSTRUCTIONS

Talk show host asks questions. Panelists respond. There are no right or wrong answers.

1. What issues are considered secretive?
2. To whom do you tell your deepest, darkest secrets?
3. Do people talk more to peers or to parents/caregivers? Explain.
4. What is an advantage of confiding in a friend?
5. What is risky about confiding in a friend?
6. Tell about a time you shared something confidential with a good friend who later spread your secret.
7. Who are trusted adults in your life?
8. What qualities are needed in a trusted adult in whom you confide?
9. What is an advantage of discussing issues with a non-family trusted adult?
10. What is a disadvantage of discussing issues with a non-family trusted adult?
11. What is professional confidentiality?
12. What situations will a professional not keep secret?
13. What older member of your family can you trust with inside information?
14. What is an advantage of confiding in an older family member?
15. What is a disadvantage of confiding in an older family member?
16. What is your opinion of people who gossip about former friends' private lives?

Consider this quote by Khalil Gibran.

If you reveal your secrets to the wind, you should not blame the wind for revealing them to the trees.

17. Who is your wind?
18. Who are your trees?

Consider this quote by Cassandra Clare.

Lies and secrets…are like cancer in the soul. They eat away what is good and leave only destruction behind.

19. Why is it important to confide in someone?
20. Whom can you trust to confide in? Why?

TEENS – Relationships with People, Places and Things

Tell and Trust
FOR THE FACILITATOR

I. Purpose
To identify trusted adults in whom teens can confide.

II. General Comments
Teens may tell secrets to today's friends who turn against them tomorrow and breach their trust.

III. Possible Activities
a. Ideally, ask teens the day before session to bring some costumes or disguises, hats, bow-ties, mustaches, sunglasses, etc. or procure these from the theater arts department.
b. Explain teens will simulate a talk show; recruit a volunteer for the host; remaining teens are panelists. Give panelists paper and tape to make name tags e.g. Professor Know-It-All.
c. Host reads the instructions aloud, then asks questions and calls on panelists to respond.
   Possible responses to elicit:
   1. Crushes, sex, pregnancy, substances, possibly serious issues like suicide or homicide
   2. Responses will be individualized
   3. Usually talk more to peers because parents/caregivers may seem judgmental
   4. A same age friend may seem to understand and not judge
   5. The friend may not always be your friend and then may not keep information private
   6. Responses will be individualized
   7. Teachers, counselors, grandparents, parents, aunts/uncles, doctors, therapists, nurses, etc.
   8. Wisdom to know when to keep a secret and when to alert someone of danger
   9. The adult is less likely to spread gossip among your peers
   10. The adult may give advice you'd rather not hear
   11. The duty to keep information private, upheld by many mental and physical health professionals, lawyers, etc.
   12. Plans or acts involving harm to self, others, domestic violence, child abuse, sexual abuse, etc.
   13. Responses will be individualized
   14. They probably feel love and concern for you
   15. They may reveal some things to parents/caregivers or other family members
   16. People who spread secrets are dishonorable, disrespectful, not true friends
   17. The wind may be people who are not trustworthy; friends today and not friends tomorrow
   18. The trees may be nosey people who want to know gossip
   19. Sharing secrets with the right person can stop the self-destruction, relieve guilt, save your life
   20. Responses will be individualized; ideally teens identify a trusted adult

IV. Enrichment Activities
a. Emphasize that most professionals and adult family members are to be trusted but also remind group that sexual predators are not always strangers.
b. Ask teens to brainstorm signs that an adult may not be trustworthy.
   Possibilities
   - Wants an exclusive relationship; discourages teen from communicating with parents/caregivers
   - Isolates the teen; finds ways to be alone
   - Expects teens to keep aspects of their relationship secret
   - Eventually makes sexual comments and advances
c. Encourage teens to honor their gut instincts – if a person seems questionable, the person may be questionable.

My Relationships with Family/People at Home

Fridge Magnet Forgiveness

Title _____

Choose love over hate.

Wipe clean the slate.

Make up before it's too late.

Title _____

Hold resentment?

Find contentment?

Make the choice.

Find your voice.

Title _____

Some hold a grudge.

They will not budge.

Their wounds they lick.

It makes them sick.

Discover a way.

To say, "It's ok."

Title _____

Not related by blood or bone.

We live together in this home.

We shout and pout

Title _____

Our blood and flesh

Remain enmeshed.

Our DNA

Won't save the day.

We decide to forgive.

That's how we live.

And hash it out.

We bare our souls

Give up control

And in the end

We love as friends.

TEENS – Relationships with People, Places and Things

Fridge Magnet Forgiveness
FOR THE FACILITATOR

I. Purpose
To choose to forgive family members, caregivers and others with whom teens reside.

II. General Comments
Refrigerator magnets convey meaningful messages. Teens create forgiveness poems to post at home.

III. Possible Activities
- a. Before session decide whether to select the Team or Individual Format.
- b. Photocopy the *Fridge Forgiveness* handout; make five copies for teams or one for each individual.
- c. Cut out the boxes, including the blanks; scramble so they are in random order, **keep the cutouts for each page in separate stacks or envelopes**; teens will later put poetry lines together like puzzle pieces. Alternatively, a volunteer cuts, scrambles and stacks the cutouts before session, or teens cut out their own pages, scramble, and set aside the stacks on their desks or table for later.
- d. At start of session, ask teens who are familiar with refrigerator poetry magnet kits to describe them.
- e. If no participants have seen the kits, ask them to imagine the kit's contents (words and phrases to be put together in any combination; magnets on the back allow them to be attached to the fridge).
- f. Explain that teens will work with poetry lines that could become fridge magnets.

  Team Format
  - Distribute one stack (the full page of scrambled cutouts) to each team.
  - Ask teams to arrange the lines into five rhyming poems.
  - Prompt teams to create a title for each poem.
  - Encourage teams to share their arrangements and titles. The uncut page shows the suggested order but any combination is acceptable.
  - Direct teams to use their blank cutouts to compose poem lines about family forgiveness.
  - Advise each team to elect a recorder to write their verses on the blank cutouts.
  - Ask recorders to scramble and stack their poetry lines.
  - Tell teams to exchange stacks and arrange each other's lines into poems.
  - Encourage teams to share their arrangements, which may or may not match the original poems.

  Individual Format
  - Distribute one stack (the full page of scrambled cutouts) to each person.
  - Ask individuals to arrange the lines into five rhyming poems.
  - Prompt teens to create a title for each poem.
  - Encourage teens share their arrangements and titles.
  - The uncut page shows the suggested order but any combination is acceptable.
  - Direct individuals to use their blank cutouts to compose poem lines about family forgiveness.
  - Ask each teen to scramble and stack their poetry lines.
  - Tell teens to exchange stacks with a nearby person and arrange each other's lines into poems.
  - Encourage teens to share their arrangements that may or may not match the original poems.

  For Both Formats
  Promote a project – provide small magnets for teens to glue to the backs of their poems for the fridge.

IV. Enrichment Activities
Start a fridge magnet fund-raiser – teens create magnet messages and sell for their schools or teams.

My Relationships with Family / People at Home

Fam-Lingo Bingo

Apply the *lingo*, a set of terms, related to your home life.

B 1-10	I 11-20	N 21-30	G 31-40	O 41-50
☐ Explain how some parents/caregivers can tend toward **strictness** or **leniency**.	☐ Share ways parents/caregivers **stand back** or **hover**.	☐ In what ways are parents/caregivers too **demanding** or too **undemanding**?	☐ In what ways do parents/caregivers **over-organize** or **limit** activities?	☐ In what ways is **respect** or **disrespect** predominant in a family?
☐ How can parents/caregivers' **expectations** be in line with teens' **maturity levels**?	☐ In what ways is a home environment **emotionally safe** or **unsafe**?	☐ Give examples of **emotional intimacy** or **distance** among family members.	☐ In what ways is the need for **privacy** upheld or ignored in a family?	☐ Describe the level of **accountability** among family members.
☐ Describe different ways family members can be **abusive**.	☐ What are some family views about **expressing** or **suppressing** feelings?	☐ In what ways can a family use or avoid **labels** regarding its family members?	☐ What does it mean to **parent** a parent/caregiver?	☐ Describe the level of **control** parents/caregivers can exert over decision-making.
☐ What relationship problems arise when a family member has an **addiction**?	☐ Describe ways a home life can be **chaotic** or **calm**.	☐ In what ways do family members show their **trust** or **distrust** of each other?	☐ In what ways do family members tend to **forgive** or **hold grudges**?	☐ Give examples of how **rigid** or **flexible** the rules can be in a family.
☐ Share ways teens tend to be too **clingy** or too **independent** in a family.	☐ In what ways can family members **build up** or **tear down** each other?	☐ Privately write an example of how **keeping family secrets** can be destructive.	☐ Give examples of the different types or levels of **resiliency** among family members.	☐ How can a family handle **conflict** among its members?

© 2014 WHOLE PERSON ASSOCIATES, 101 W. 2ND ST., SUITE 203, DULUTH MN 55802 • 800-247-6789

TEENS – Relationships with People, Places and Things

Fam-Lingo Bingo
FOR THE FACILITATOR

I. Purpose
To consider family relationship issues that affect teens.

II. General Comments
Through an individual activity or game, teens identify possible attitudes and behaviors in families.

III. Possible Activities
  a. Before session decide whether to use the handout as an individual activity or BINGO game.
    Individual Activity Option
- Photocopy the *Fam-Lingo BINGO* handout and distribute the page to participants.
- Ask teens to write their personalized responses on a separate page, based on their own family or home life.
- Ask for volunteers to share their responses within their comfort zone.

    BINGO Game Option
- Distribute the page; explain that teens will play BINGO by responding aloud to the questions.
- Direct teens to number their squares based on the numbers at the top of each column.
- Teens need to number their squares differently.
  Example
- Under "B" one teen uses 1, 2, 3, 4, 5; another uses 6, 7, 8, 9, 10; another uses 1, 3, 5, 7, 9, etc.
- Facilitator may use the grid below to record numbers in each square as they are called.

B 1-10	I 11-20	N 21-30	G 31-40	O 41-50

- Facilitator calls numbers under each letter respectively.
- Teens with that letter and number raise their hands and take turns responding aloud.
- As they respond, they shade in the squares on their handouts.
- Teens write their response to the question about family secrets and need not share.
- If teens do not understand a question or cannot answer, peers may assist.
- If the same players have lots of turns, ask teens who have had few turns to call the next numbers.
- Teens win by accruing a shaded row of horizontal, vertical or diagonal squares.
- As teens win, they take turns being the caller, then return to their seats and continue playing.
- The game continues until everyone has shaded all squares (Black-Out BINGO).

  b. During or after the individual activity or BINGO game, reinforce concepts:
- Emotional safety involves freedom to express feelings (respectfully).
- With addiction, life revolves around the addict, roles change, secrets and unpredictability prevail.
- Resilience is the ability of the family unit and its members to bounce back after a crisis.
- To handle conflict in a healthy way includes sharing feelings, listening, reaching compromises.

IV. Enrichment Activities
  a. Brainstorm with group some of the ways teens can overcome unhealthy patterns, e.g. ways to become less clingy, build up versus tear down, respect others, forgive, etc.
  b. Reinforce issues that require professional intervention: abuse, addiction, severe conflict, etc.

MY RELATIONSHIPS WITH PEERS

Fear makes strangers of people who would be friends.
~ Shirley MacLaine

Shape-ing Friendships .... page 29 ▶
Teens view overlapping circles, a triangle and a sun with its rays to illustrate friendship dynamics.
Teens minimize jealousy and enmeshment and maximize social supports and personal development.

Friends and Cliques .... page 31 ▶
Teens determine the benefits of individual friends and/or healthy cliques versus involvement in unhealthy cliques. Teens consider how someone who feels alone can make friends and how peers can include the person.

Quote Apps .... page 33 ▶
Teens apply modern and classic quotations to their friendships.
Teens ponder telling the truth, growing separately without growing apart, caring but not owning.

Afraid of Missing Out? .... page 35 ▶
Teens are helped to overcome excessive social concerns and to prioritize safety and balance.
Teens note that dangerous risks, too many activities, jealousy, and constant connection are unnecessary.

Inclusion Pantomimes .... page 37 ▶
Teens present pantomimes to portray the pain of exclusion and ways to include peers.
Teens discuss reactions of people who have experienced exclusion and potentially tragic outcomes.

Play Ball? .... page 39 ▶
Teens view a ball game and consider possible motives and traits of people who reject others.
Teens identify ways to be a part of a positive peer group.

Embarrassment Happens .... pages 41–44 ▶
Teens contemplate ways to handle embarrassing situations with grace and tact.
Teens acknowledge how their words and actions affect themselves and others.

Cookie Cutter Categories .... page 45 ▶
Teens recognize that the word "the" unfairly categorizes people.
Teens celebrate people's uniqueness and do not define them by a perceived difference or disability.

The Marks Humans Leave .... page 47 ▶
Teens develop empathy for victims of bullying or other forms of emotional cruelty.
Teens decide to leave marks of hope and healing rather than inflicting painful scars.

My Relationships with Peers

Shape-ing Friendships

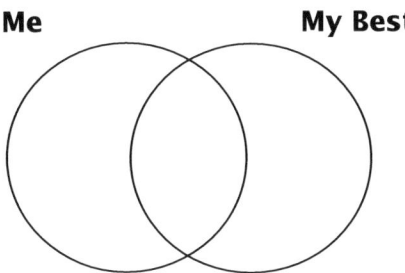
Me — My Best Friend

1. Write your common interests where the circles overlap and separate interests near the circumferences.
2. What is an advantage of the above relationship? _____
3. What is a disadvantage? _____

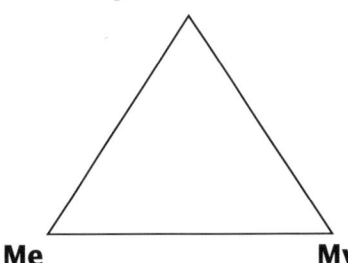
My Best Friend
Me — My Best Friend's New Friend

4. How would it feel if your best friendship became a triangle?
_____

5. Label the sun (circle) *"Me"*.
6. Label one of the sun's rays as *"Best Friend."*
7. Label three of the sun's rays as supportive people in your life (use name codes).
8. Label one of the sun's rays as an activity you enjoy.
9. Label one of the sun's rays as an activity important to your future.
10. Label one of the sun's rays as your source of spiritual support or inner strength.
11. Label one of the sun's rays as a cause you believe in strongly.
12. Which shape (circle, triangle or sun) is best for you? _____

Explain _____
_____

TEENS – Relationships with People, Places and Things

Shape-ing Friendships

FOR THE FACILITATOR

I. Purpose
To decrease jealousy related to best friendships.
To minimize enmeshment and maximize social supports and personal development.

II. General Comments
Teens may feel possessiveness toward best friends and fear losing the relationship. As teens expand their support system and pursue productive activities the intensity diminishes; the friendship is put into perspective amidst other sources of satisfaction.

III. Possible Activities
   a. Ask teens *"What is the shape of friendship?"* Invite them to draw diagrams on the board and elaborate.
   b. Distribute the *Shape-ing Friendships* handout; allow time for completion; (teens use name codes).
   c. Encourage teens to share their responses.
   Possibilities:
   1. Responses will be individualized.
   2. One advantage is closeness.
   3. One disadvantage is that one may be partly over-shadowed by the other.
   4. A teen might feel jealous – fearful the new friend will *steal* the best friend.
   5. Each teen is the center of his/her life for purposes of the diagram.
   6. To label one ray as *Best Friend* shows that the best friend is one of many sources of support.
   7. Teens identify supportive people (friends, family, teachers, coaches, spiritual advisors).
   8. Sports, music, art, journaling, crafts, TV, movies, can be done with or without the best friend.
   9. Education, volunteer or paid work, etc. enhance self-development apart from the best friend.
   10. Meditation, nature's beauty, solitude, prayer, inspirational literature, etc. inspire; teens need not turn to the best friend for everything.
   11. Teens involved in human rights, political, environmental or other concerns are usually less possessive of friends because they have other things to think about.
   12. Teens will hopefully see the sun as a whole, rays and all, as the best possible support system.
   13. Explain: The sun shows an array of people, including the best friend, rather than one friendship.

IV. Enrichment Activities
   a. Encourage a discussion regarding whether to tell the best friend about feelings of jealousy or to tell a trusted adult (answers will vary).
   b. Ask teens to identify traits that lead to possessiveness (fear of losing the best friend, low self-esteem, a history of being abandoned or replaced in relationships, immaturity, control issues).
   c. Discuss scenarios:
      - You have a best friend and a new friend – how do you handle possible rivalry?
        (Don't brag about one's qualities to the other; avoid inside jokes that cause one to feel left out; do things with each separately but also do some activities with the three of you or with a group of friends).
      - Picture yourself as being the new friend – how do you handle the older friend's resentment?
        (Don't react in anger; try to be friendly and show interest in the person).
   d. Ask teens to share their experiences regarding friendship, concerns, fears and/or jealousy; and to receive peer feedback.

My Relationships with Peers

Friends and Cliques

Friends – No Clique	Healthy Clique	Unhealthy Clique
Free to be one's own person	Free to be own person and be in a clique	Blurred individuality
Open to everyone	Have friends in and outside of the clique	Friends with ONLY clique members
Individual thinking	Learn from others & think for self	Conform to other clique members
Kind	Kind to clique members and others	Unkind, mean and/or bully others
Free to be friends with anyone	Clique is open and welcomes others	Excludes others
Friendly	Friendly with clique members and others	Hostile to others
Welcomes people not especially like oneself	Welcomes different people to group	Rejects people who are different in any way
Helpful to everyone	Helpful to clique members and others	Harmful to members and outsiders
Trustworthy	Trust among clique members and others	Lie, manipulate, double-cross, gossip, put people down and/or relay rumors
Supportive	Supportive of clique members and friends	Individuals desperate for members' approval, at any cost
Secure about friendships	Secure inside and outside clique	Insecure inside and outside clique
Accepting	Accepting of clique members and others	Rejecting and controlling
Does not judge friends	Does not judge members or others	Judgmental
Equality	Equality for clique members and others	False superiority
Have friends' backs	Have clique members' and others' backs in a healthy way	Have clique members' backs, only if members conform
Have friends to go to	Have friends and clique members to go to	Have clique members to go to, only if one conforms
Have good friends	Have a sense of belonging	Sense of belonging conditionally
Suggestions and good advice	Suggestions and good advice	Negative peer-pressure
Able to make new friends	Able to make new friends for self and clique members	Closed off from other people
Own person	No particular leader	Leader who might be mean, hostile, bully
Independent	Interdependence among members	Dependent on approval
Other		
Other		

1. On the above table, circle the column heading that best describes your social network.
2. Would you like to be in a different network? _____ Explain: _____

_____

3. If you disagree with any of the descriptors place a check mark on the boxes and explain your reasons on the back of this page.
4. If you know of additional descriptors, add them in the blank boxes.

TEENS – Relationships with People, Places and Things

Friends and Cliques
FOR THE FACILITATOR

I. Purpose
To identify benefits of friendships and healthy cliques and the negative aspects of unhealthy cliques.

II. General Comments
A sense of belonging to a peer group may be important to some teens; teens will recognize that cliques with members who reject, control, judge, bully, etc. are detrimental to their own members and to outsiders.

III. Possible Activities
   a. Before session decide on Team Format or Poster Activity; (make cutouts for Poster Activity; headings on notebook paper for Team Format).
   b. Write *Clique* on the board; ask its meaning (a close circle of people, similar interests and goals).
   c. Ask if cliques are positive or negative (they can be either depending on their focus).
   d. Ask teens for examples of harmful cliques (gangs; groups who bully).
   e. Ask teens for examples of helpful cliques (friends who encourage individuality, build up each other and encourage members to have friends outside of the clique).
   f. Ask the value of having friends but not being in a clique (a variety of supportive people).

   Poster Activity
   - Before session photocopy the *Friends and Cliques* handout; cut out or recruit a volunteer to cut out all the descriptor boxes. Scramble the cutouts and place in a pile at the front of the room.
   - On large poster paper head columns: *Friends – No Clique, Healthy Clique, Unhealthy Clique.*
   - Teens take turns: pick up a cutout, read aloud, decide with peers in which column it belongs, and tape it under the heading. (The handout suggests placement, but allow teens to discuss and debate.) Display the finished poster for students in other classes to view.
   - Distribute copies of the uncut handout; allow time to complete the questions at the bottom.
   - Encourage teens to share their responses and receive peer feedback.

   Team Format
   - Write headings on the board: *Friends- No Clique, Healthy Clique, Unhealthy Clique.*
   - Elicit an example of a characteristic for each (use the *Friends and Cliques* page as a resource but do not yet give it to teens).
   - Divide teens into three teams; give each team a piece of notebook paper with one of the headings (*Friends – No Clique; Healthy Clique; Unhealthy Clique*).
   - Teammates sit together; each team designates a writer to list their ideas.
   - Explain that teams will identify as many characteristics as possible for their category.
   - Circulate among the teams; assist as needed and reinforce when teens are on track.
   - Teens reconvene; writers take turns reading aloud and/or listing their teammates' ideas on the board.
   - Encourage teens from other teams to provide feedback and add ideas.
   - Distribute the *Friends and Cliques* handout; teens take turns reading aloud each line from left to right (to compare the descriptors for each concept).
   - Encourage teens to elaborate on their related experiences.
   - Allow time to complete the questions at the bottom.
   - Encourage teens to share responses including items they added and those with which they disagree

IV. Enrichment Activities
   a. Encourage teens to consider one more alternative: Write on the board *People with No Friends*.
   b. Ask what qualities might cause teens to have no friends (shyness, having a noticeable difference, being outcast by bullies; vicious gossip, an unfavorable reputation, rudeness, conceit, aggressiveness, etc.).
   c. Ask what a teen with no friends might do (volunteer at a charity, join a club; change negative behavior).
   d. Ask what peers can do to help people who feel alone (smile, speak, invite them to *hang out* with friends, ask for their opinions or for their help on a project, etc.).

My Relationships with Peers ▶

Quote Apps

Modern Quotations ↓

1. All you have to do to be my friend is like me.
~ Taylor Swift

2. A friend can tell you things you don't want to tell yourself. ~ Frances Ward Weller

3. The most beautiful discovery true friends can make is that they can grow separately without growing apart. ~ Elisabeth Foley

4. For me, a quarterback's best friend, especially a young quarterback's best friend, is a coach who believes in him. ~ Robert Griffin III

5. You can't make someone be your best friend.
~ Rosalind Wiseman

6. The biggest ingredient in a best friend is someone whose actions you respect and who you can truly be yourself around.
~ Renee Olstead

Classic Quotations ↓

1. Friendship with one's self is all important because without it one cannot be friends with anyone else in the world.
~ Eleanor Roosevelt

2. Friendship is held to be the severest test of character. ~ Charles Eastman

3. Sometimes you put up walls not to keep people out, but to see who cares enough to break them down. ~ Socrates

4. I do not need a friend who changes when I change and who nods when I nod; my shadow does that much better. ~ Plutarch

5. Caring for but never trying to own may be a further way to define friendship.
~ William Glasser

6. Music is the social act of communication among people, a gesture of friendship, the strongest there is. ~ Malcolm Arnold.

Insert the number for the most meaningful modern and classic quotation and elaborate.

Modern Quote # _____ means most to me ...	Classic Quote # _____ means most to me ...

TEENS – Relationships with People, Places and Things

Quote Apps
FOR THE FACILITATOR

I. Purpose
   To apply modern and classic quotations to teen friendship; to examine and compose words of wisdom and song lyrics about friendship.

II. General Comments
   Teens may be more receptive to modern public figures' beliefs but will also consider ageless ideas.

III. Possible Activities
   a. Write *Friendship past and present* on the board; ask teens if they think friends felt the same about each other a hundred years ago as they do today (encourage discussion; there are no right or wrong answers).
   b. Distribute the *Quote Apps* handout; teens read the quotations and directions aloud.
   c. Allow time for completion.
   d. Encourage teens to share their responses regarding their most meaningful quotes.
   e. Ask questions below that correspond to the quotation numbers; possible ideas to elicit are parenthesized.

   Modern Quotations
   1. What do some people do to get friends? (pretend to be something they are not or do something they do not want to do).
   2. What truth would you tell a friend, even if the person denies it? (speak out if you see signs of addiction).
   3. How can friends grow separately but not drift apart? (talk or write to each other about their pursuits).
   4. In sports or in life, what does a coach do? (teaches, motivates, believes in each person).
   5. Why can't you force friendship? (you can't control people's feelings).
   6. What kinds of actions will people respect? (loyalty, kindness, generosity, honesty).

   Classic Quotations
   1. How can you be a friend to yourself? (act according to your beliefs).
   2. In what ways are people tempted to betray friends? (gossip about them).
   3. How do you start to break down walls? (smile, speak, listen, include, help).
   4. Why not agree with everything a friend does? (a true friend will value your views).
   5. How do you not *own* a friend? (Have other interests and friends, accept and respect the friend's different interests, beliefs, etc.).
   6. In addition to music, what are other social acts of communication? (prose, poetry, art, theater, social media).

IV. Enrichment Activities
   a. Ask teens to share other sayings they have heard about friends and friendship.
   b. Encourage teens to write and then share their own words of wisdom on the topic.
   c. Suggest that teens find friendship quotes in popular music lyrics, copy them and then share with the group; set ground rules, e.g., no profanity or harm.
   d. Encourage teens to compose their own song lyrics about friendship.
   e. Prompt teens to agree, disagree, discuss and debate about messages in the sayings and lyrics.

My Relationships with Peers

Afraid of Missing Out?

Are you afraid of missing out? Do you ...

- Worry that others are having fun without you?
- Take risks to be with people you want to accept you?
- Overwhelm yourself with too many activities?
- Feel jealous when you see others' popularity and possessions?
- Stay connected to people 24/7 because someone might need you?
- Change yourself to fit in?
- Worry about how others will judge you for doing what you want – being your own person?

Put yourself in these scenarios.

1. You're invited to a party by a friend who drinks and drives; other peers have no cars. What do you do?

2. You're driving and receive a call from someone you've been waiting to hear from? What do you do?

3. You need to prepare a report for class tomorrow. Your friends are going to a concert tonight. What do you do?

4. You are exhausted and need time alone. Friends pressure you to be with them. What do you do?

5. You haven't been invited to a friend's party. Other friends will be there. What do you do?

People who do things because they're afraid of missing out, often miss out on other things that are way more important.

What might you miss out on if you ...

6. Get in a car with a driver who has been drinking?

7. Take on too much?

8. Try to keep up with others?

TEENS – Relationships with People, Places and Things

Afraid of Missing Out?
FOR THE FACILITATOR

I. Purpose
To overcome excessive social concerns; to prioritize safety and balance.

II. General Comments
Teens often want to be liked, accepted and included.

III. Possible Activities
   a. Write on the board *Afraid of Missing Out?*
   b. Ask teens what they fear missing out on (parties, fun with friends, sports teams or events, etc.)
   c. Distribute the *Afraid of Missing Out?* handout; teens read aloud the text box information.
   d. Allow time for completion then encourage teens to share responses.
      Possibilities correspond to numbers on the handout:
      1. Ask parent/caregiver to drive you or check the public transportation schedule.
      2. Pull over if safe to do so; call back or text as soon as you reach your destination.
      3. Prepare the report tonight and plan a weekend activity with friends.
      4. Explain you need some time to recharge.
      5. Ask the person why.
      6. You might miss out on life and health if killed or disabled in a crash.
      7. You might not do your best if you spread yourself too thin.
      8. You might lose your own identity and forget who you really are.
   e. Encourage teens to identify ways to achieve balance in their lives (set times for technology, socializing, study, work, family; take time for solitude and spirituality).
   f. Ask teens whether people who fear missing out are more or less likely to text while driving (more).
   g. Ask what teens who text and drive may miss out on (life and limb).
   h. Ask teens to identify ways to be **emotionally** connected rather than solely electronically connected (through satisfying paid or volunteer work, true friends, loving partners, a genuine support system).

IV. Enrichment Activities
Encourage teens to elaborate upon these ideas:
   - How satisfied are people who obsess about missing out? (Generally dissatisfied because they are convinced there is always something or someone better, but beyond their reach).
   - Are people's images and activities on social media real or fake? (Images are enhanced and people tend to exaggerate and brag).
   - How might technology make people think they are missing out? (With a touch of the finger they see friends having fun, glamorous places, expensive *toys*, people's boy/girlfriends, etc.).
   - What happens when teens are available to everyone night and day? (Burnout; they may feel needed but may be of little help to people if they take no time to personally rejuvenate physically and mentally).

My Relationships with Peers

Inclusion Pantomimes

(4 actors)

1. Three people form a circle and hold hands. A fourth person stands outside and looks in.

(3 actors)

2. Two teens are talking. A third teen walks up to them.

(5 actors)

3. Three teens point and laugh at a fourth teen who has fallen and can't get up. A fifth teen observes.

(6 actors)

4. Four teens stand next to each other raising their hands as if asking to be chosen. A leader chooses three; three teens and leader walk away with arms around each other. An onlooker observes the one left behind.

(4 actors)

5. Three teens sit in a circle eating. Another sits a few feet away eating alone.

(5 actors)

6. A few teens are dancing. One teen sits on the sidelines.

(4 actors)

7. A teen is driving with a couple of passengers. A teen the driver knows is at the side of the road, waving arms to flag them down.

(3 actors)

8. Two teens sit together with textbooks open, writing on paper as if helping each other study. A third teen sits nearby and crumples a paper in frustration.

© 2014 WHOLE PERSON ASSOCIATES, 101 W. 2ND ST., SUITE 203, DULUTH MN 55802 • 800-247-6789

TEENS – Relationships with People, Places and Things

Inclusion Pantomimes

FOR THE FACILITATOR

I. Purpose
To motivate teens to include peers and understand the pain of being excluded.

II. General Comments
Teens present pantomimes to illustrate inclusion.

III. Possible Activities
    a. Before session photocopy the *Inclusion Pantomimes* handout and cut-out scripts on the broken lines.
    b. Place scripts face down on a table in front of the room.
    c. Write on the board *Inclusion* and *Exclusion* and ask teens their meanings (to bring in or keep out).
    d. Ask teens to raise their hands if they have ever felt left out.
    e. Ask teens to raise their hands if they have ever kept someone out of a group.
    f. Encourage teens to share experiences within their comfort zones and to use name codes.
    g. Explain that they will perform *pantomimes* of situations where people are excluded or in danger of being rejected; emphasize that actions, not words, are required.
    h. Teen actors will welcome a newcomer or help a person who is treated like an outcast.
    i. A teen goes to the front of the room, picks up the top script and asks for the specified number of actors. The teen must remember to count self as one of the actors.
    j. The actors huddle briefly to decide on roles and actions; then portray the scene.
    k. The actors decide in advance or ad lib regarding how the inclusion or helping will occur.
    l. Teens take turn pantomiming the situations; audience peers give feedback after each performance.
    m. Teens figure out their own ways to include or comfort a potential outcast; some possibilities:
        1. Teens create an opening in the circle for the newcomer by waving to the person to join (physically illustrates inclusion).
        2. Teens acknowledge the newcomer with a smile (rather than ignoring the person).
        3. The observer (fifth teen) helps the person up (shows willingness to help a person).
        4. The onlooker might shake hands (shows empathy).
        5. The teens eating together gesture to the lone teen to join them (shows inclusion).
        6. One of the dancing teens takes the person onto the dance floor (shows awareness that someone might not be having a good time).
        7. The driver stops the car and gestures to the friend to get in (shows inclusion).
        8. The study partners gesture to the frustrated teen to join them (shows willingness to help).
    n. Ask the teens who portrayed the excluded persons how they felt when they were left out.
    o. Ask the teens who portrayed the excluded persons how they felt to be included.

IV. Enrichment Activities
    a. Encourage teens to write their own scripts and act out examples of inclusion or exclusion.
    b. Encourage a discussion about reactions among teens who have felt excluded (depression, anger, resentment; some have perpetrated violence like school shootings; others have committed suicide).

My Relationships with Peers

Play Ball?

Think about being in a three way game of catch.

At first the other two people toss the ball to you often.

Then they throw to each other and ignore you.

1. How do you feel? _____
_____

Re-think the situation:

2. What are some probable traits of people who exclude others? _____
_____

3, What might motivate them? _____
_____

4. What kind of people do you want to *play ball* with (or have as friends)? _____
_____

Depict and/or describe a time you felt left out.	Depict and/or describe a time when you treated someone like an outcast.

TEENS – Relationships with People, Places and Things

Play Ball?
FOR THE FACILITATOR

I. Purpose
To recognize that peers who exclude others are probably people one would not want for friends.

II. General Comments
Rejection hurts. Teens who exclude or bully often have problematic traits and motivations.

III. Possible Activities
a. If possible have a ball, beanbag, flying disc, foot bag or lightweight object available.

b. Privately coach three teens to portray this scenario:
Three teens play catch together at first; then two players throw to each other and ignore the third.

c. The actors take their seats.

d. Distribute the *Play Ball?* handout and allow time for completion.

e. Encourage teens to share their responses.
Possibilities corresponding to numbers on the handout:

1. Teens might feel sad, hurt, left out, angry, etc.

2. Traits of peers who exclude others might be a lack of empathy or compassion.

3. Possible motives: false superiority as they make others feel inferior; power and control; popularity stemming from being the *in-group*. Some teens cover insecurity by being the first to shun or tease; some have been abused and turn the tables by hurting others; they may suffer from unresolved anger, depression, etc.

4. People with common interests who promote individuality and celebrate each others' successes.

Depictions and descriptions will vary; encourage teens to process feelings and receive peer feedback. Remind teens to use name codes.

IV. Enrichment Activities
Encourage teens to discuss ways to break into a positive peer group.

Possibilities:

a. Start by talking to one person; a positive group encourages new members to join.

b. Join a service organization that helps others like food and clothing donation programs, animal shelters, etc. to meet peers who care about social, political or environmental issues.

c. Find your passion for art, writing, theater, dance, sports, etc.; join a related club or activity.

d. Join activities at a library, house of worship, Department of Parks and Recreation, etc.

My Relationships with Peers

Embarrassment Happens
I Embarrassed Myself

Share your embarrassing moments and ways you did or could have coped with each situation.

Category	How I Embarrassed Myself	How I Handled the Situation	How I Could Have Handled It Better
Example: Bodily Functions	I burped loudly in class.	I laughed nervously when people stared at me.	I just say, "Excuse me."
Bodily Functions			
Verbal			
Sports			
Technology			
Clothing			
Appearance			
Intellectual			
Emotional			
Social			
Other			
Other			

(continued)

Embarrassment Happens
I Embarrassed Someone

Category	How I Embarrassed Someone	How I Handled the Situation	How I Could Have Handled It Better
Example: Intellectual	I told people that a classmate failed a test.	I denied it when confronted.	I could have told the person that I am very sorry and I should never have told anyone.
Bodily Functions			
Verbal			
Sports			
Technology			
Clothing			
Appearance			
Intellectual			
Emotional			
Social			
Other			
Other			

(continued)

My Relationships with Peers

Embarrassment Happens
Someone Embarrassed Me

Category	How Someone Embarrassed Me	How I Handled the Situation	How I Could Have Handled It Better
Example: Appearance	A peer made fun of my hair.	I became angry and walked away.	With a smile, I could have said, "I like it that way!
Bodily Functions			
Verbal			
Sports			
Technology			
Clothing			
Appearance			
Intellectual			
Emotional			
Social			
Other			
Other			

TEENS – Relationships with People, Places and Things

Embarrassment Happens

FOR THE FACILITATOR

I. Purpose
To recognize that some embarrassing situations can be handled with grace and diplomacy.

II. General Comments
Teens consider how their words and actions affect self and others and ways to minimize damage.

III. Possible Activities
   a. Read aloud this scenario:
      "A rich teen gave a less fortunate friend a pair of shoes and then told everyone."
   b. Ask teens how they think the less fortunate teen felt (embarrassed).
   c. Ask teens to share embarrassing moments, without using names or embarrassing anyone in the room.
   d. Distribute the first *Embarrassment Happens* handout, *I Embarrassed Myself,* page 41.
   e. Ask a volunteer to read the directions and example aloud.
   f. Allow time for completion.
   g. Encourage teens to share their responses within their comfort zones without naming or embarrassing anyone.
   h. Responses will be individualized.
   i. In the same or a subsequent session(s) distribute second handout: *I Embarrassed Someone,* page 42, and the third handout: *Someone Embarrassed Me,* page 43.
   j. Repeat steps *e-g* above.
   k. Prompt teens to identify basics for dealing with an embarrassing situation.
   Possibilities
   - Admit you made a mistake.
   - Apologize sincerely (once is enough).
   - Set the record straight if you hurt someone's reputation or feelings.
   - Realize that the situation is over; let it go.
   - Learn from the incident.
   - Know that your embarrassing moment is not as big to others as it is to you.
   - Laugh at yourself.
   - Know it's ok to be human.
   - Take a time out if needed but get back in the game (don't run and hide).
   - Know that no one is perfect; everyone has embarrassing episodes.
   - Realize that someone who embarrasses you also embarrasses themself.

IV. Enrichment Activities
Encourage a discussion of ways to prevent embarrassing self and others.
Possibilities
   - If embarrassed by someone, be sure not to do or say the same thing to someone else.
   - Avoid jokes about others.
   - Avoid comments about weight, age or other traits that could be interpreted as an insult.
   - Never make ethnic, racial or cultural jokes.
   - Do not minimize people's opinions because they are younger or newer in the group.
   - Do not confront someone in front of others.
   - Do not send, write or say anything you would not want the world to know.
   - Do not lie or blame others to save yourself from embarrassment.
   - Think before you talk. Consider how you would feel if someone said to you what you are about to say.

Cookie Cutter Categories

Consider these statements:
- Give more privileges to the teens.
- Set up shelters for the homeless.
- Ensure access for the physically disabled.
- Advocate equal rights for the mentally ill.
- Don't discriminate against the minorities.
- Be friendly to the special education students.
- Create fashionable styles for the obese, the thin, the tall, the short, etc.
- Support guide dogs for the sight-impaired.
- Provide sign language interpreters for the hearing impaired.

The term "Cookie Cutter" refers to "resembling many others of the same kind."

1. What three-letter word in the list above assumes people are like cookie cutters? _____

2. What does it mean to put people in cookie cutter categories? _____

3. Re-write one of the sentences above, replacing the word "the" with "people."

    Example: Ensure access for the physically disabled.
    Changed to: Ensure access for people with a physical disability.

4. Why put the word "people" first? _____

5. In what ways are people in all of the above groups more like you than different? _____

6. Do you think that mental health or mental is illness all about the mind? _____

7. Fill in the Body and Environment boxes to show their connection to the mind/emotions.

Mind/Emotions	Body (Physical Factors)	Environment
Thoughts, moods, stress responses, etc.		

8. Instead of cookie cutter categorizing, treat others as _____ _____ !

TEENS – Relationships with People, Places and Things

Cookie Cutter Categories
FOR THE FACILITATOR

I. Purpose
To recognize that in some contexts the word "the" suggests that certain groups of people are quite possibly of a culture different than their own and less worthy; "the" can compartmentalize, stereotype and stigmatize.
To understand the mind-body-environment connection in the misnomer "mental."

II. General Comments
Teens encounter people who are often categorized and defined by one trait. Teens consider statements that seem to advocate for specific groups but actually diminish their personhood.

III. Possible Activities
  a. Before group decide whether to use actual cookie cutters and/or play dough and obtain these items.
  b. Ideally obtain same shaped cookies for purposes of illustration and as snacks to conclude the session.
  c. If possible display a few cookie cutters or cookies with defined shapes or photos of cookie cutters.
  d. Ask teens the purpose for cookie cutters (to make cookies with the same shapes and sizes).
  e. If available, distribute many of the same shaped cookie cutters and play dough.
     Allow teens to cut out and display their play dough cookies.
     Ask what happened (all of the cookies look alike).
  f. Distribute the *Cookie Cutter Categories* handout; encourage teens to notice the art work.
  g. Volunteers read the statements aloud; then allow time for completion of numbers 1-8.
  h. Encourage teens to share their responses.
     Possibilities
     1. "the"
     2. to lump everyone together without recognizing their individuality
     3. Any sentence using "people with," or "people who are," etc.
     4. Because everyone is a person first, has many individual traits, and is not defined by only one characteristic.
     5. They all have likes, dislikes, hopes, dreams; they need to be loved, to belong, and to reach their maximum potentials.
     6. No, most wellness and illnesses encompass mind-body-environmental connections.
     7. See below

Mind/Emotions	Body (Physical Factors)	Environment
Thoughts, moods, stress response, etc.	Genetics Brain chemicals Exposure to mind-altering substances, etc.	Nurturing or neglect Physical, emotional, sexual abuse Severe conflict or cooperation, etc.

     8. People first, human beings, unique individuals, etc.
  i. If available, distribute actual cookies for the teens to enjoy.

IV. Enrichment Activities
  a. Encourage teens who are willing to share their experiences with being stereotyped or by unfairly categorizing others.
  b. Motivate teens to create posters, drawings, slogans or poems that refute stereotypes or that address individual needs.
     - Illustrate the damaging effects of compartmentalizing people
     - Celebrate each person's uniqueness
     - Emphasize the commonalities among people who also have differences

My Relationships with Peers

The Marks Humans Leave

The marks humans leave are too often scars. ~ John Green

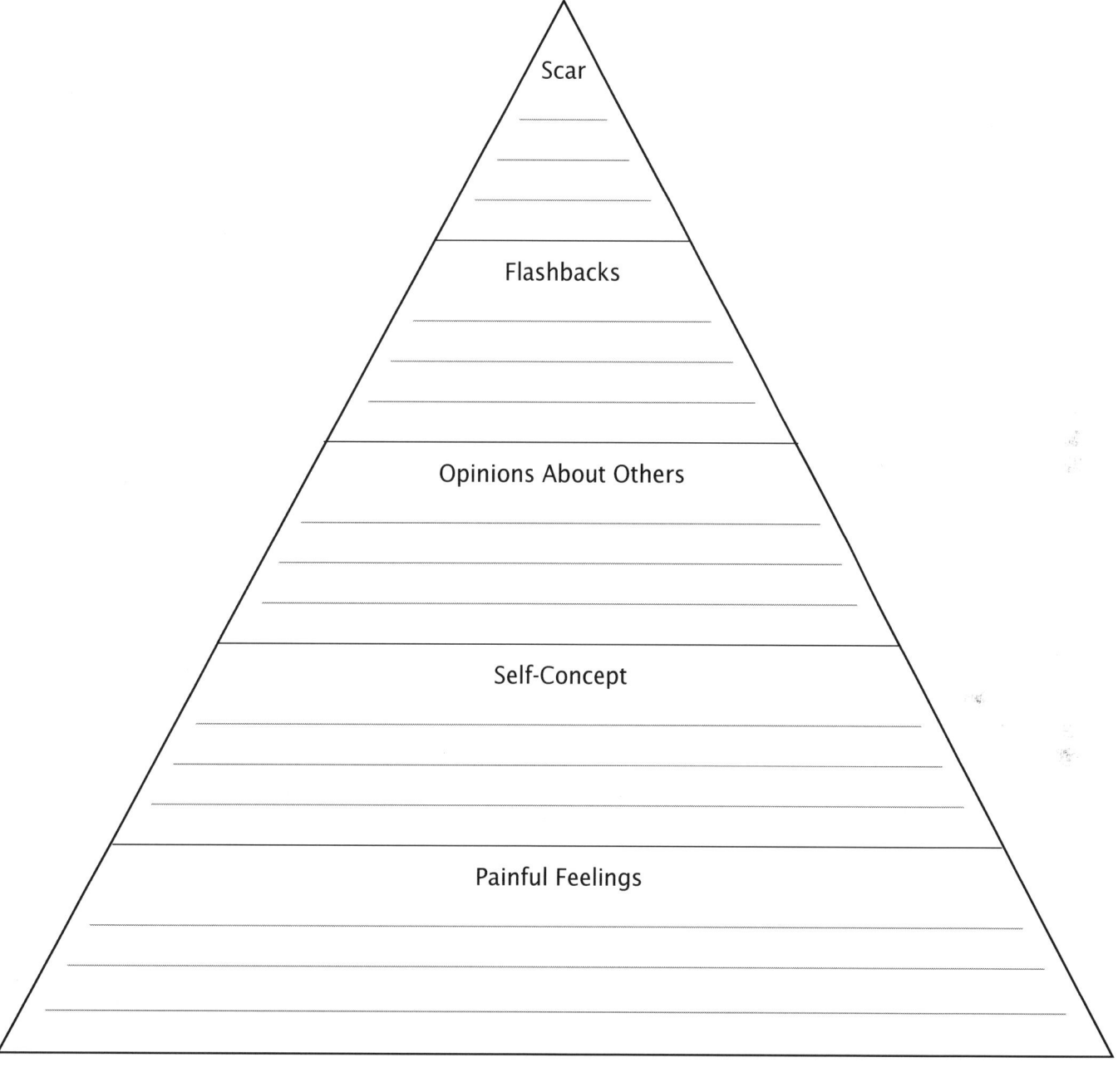

- Scar
- Flashbacks
- Opinions About Others
- Self-Concept
- Painful Feelings

In the diagram above, add your ideas about what happens with an invisible scar. What kind of marks do you want to leave?

_____
_____

TEENS – Relationships with People, Places and Things

The Marks Humans Leave

FOR THE FACILITATOR

I. Purpose
To develop empathy for victims of bullying or other forms of emotional cruelty; to decide to *leave marks of hope and healing* rather than inflicting pain.

II. General Comments
Teens may gossip about, ignore, or otherwise emotionally, physically, sexually, verbally and/or mentally hurt peers. Invisible scars have caused suicides, homicides and other miseries.

III. Possible Activities
   a. Instruct each teen to take a piece of notebook paper, crumple it without tearing, and stomp on it.
   b. Tell teens to unfold and attempt to smooth out their papers.
      Elicit that the papers have wrinkles and smudges that cannot be removed.
   c. Direct teens to tell their wrinkled papers they are sorry for messing them up.
   d. Ask if their apologies fixed the papers (no).
   e. Encourage teens to make analogies between the wrinkled papers and emotional scars left by cruelty.
   f. Distribute *The Marks Humans Leave* handout; a volunteer reads the quotation aloud.
   g. Ask teens to think about a time when they were hurt in some way.
      Elicit
      - The scar may be how they act outwardly.
      - Flashbacks may contain hurtful or painful be memories of the event.
      - Opinions about others may be generalizations based on how they were hurt.
      - Self-concepts may be low due to the situation.
      - Painful feelings may be buried underneath.
   h. Allow time for completion.
   i. Encourage teens to share their responses and receive peer feedback.
      Possibilities of a person being bullied:
      - Scar: withdrawn, isolative, suicidal or homicidal behavior.
      - Flashbacks: indelible memories of the aggressors' faces, words and actions.
      - Opinions about Others: may see everyone as mean and untrustworthy.
      - Self-concept: may believe the bullies and see themselves as *worthless, ugly, stupid, weird.*
      - Painful Feelings: invisible, wish to be invisible, self-hatred, shame, sadness, rage, fear, hopelessness, emptiness, numbness.
      - What kind of mark do you want to leave? Hope, healing, compassion, inclusion, advocacy.

IV. Enrichment Activities
   a. Discuss the fact that people who have been hurt often become isolated because peers do not want to be linked with them; elicit the importance of befriending and advocating for peers who are excluded.
   b. Emphasize that we never want to inflict scars and teens who have been hurt can heal.
   c. Encourage teens to make posters about how to leave marks of hope and healing.
   d. Discuss the concept that scar tissue is stronger then regular tissue.
   e. Ask teens to brainstorm how victims can become survivors.
      Possibilities
      - Understand that abusers may have been abused and may try to elevate themselves by putting others down and/or abusing others.
      - Process feelings with a counselor, trusted adult and/or spiritual leader.
      - Know that name-calling words do not define you.
      - Use positive self-talk.

MY RELATIONSHIPS WITH ROMANTIC PARTNERS 3

Tell me who admires you and loves you, and I will tell you who you are.
~ Charles Augustin Sainte-Beuve

Loves Me, Loves Me Not .... page 51 ▶
Teens examine aspects of romance, and differentiate between healthy and unhealthy relationships. Teens identify attributes that lead to positive partnerships.

BitterSweet Dating Violence .... page 53 ▶
Teens recognize the cycle of dating violence and learn to stop the abuse or leave the relationship. Teens consider power and control, and verbal, emotional, physical and sexual abuse.

Costs and Benefits .... page 55 ▶
Teens evaluate emotional, physical, social, financial, intellectual, sexual and other costs of a relationship. Teens define costs that are too high under any circumstances – abuse, health or safety risks, etc.

Amusement Park Analogies .... page 57 ▶
Teens express thoughts and feelings about romance and compare them to amusement park rides. Teens discover ways to stay emotionally and physically safe in relationships.

Does Break Up = Broken Heart? .... page 59 ▶
Teens change devastating thoughts about a break up and learn they can emerge stronger and wiser. Teens identify signs in themselves or peers that suggest the need of help from a trusted adult.

Leave Respectfully .... page 61 ▶
Teens differentiate between respectful and disrespectful ways to initiate a break up. Teens brainstorm ways the other partner can handle the break up with self-respect and emotional stability.

Romantic Jealousy: The Other Side of the Coin .... page 63 ▶
Teens are helped to understand that irrational or unwarranted jealousy is related to their own insecurities, and they brainstorm ways to counteract jealousy. Teens recognize that attraction can't be forced or earned.

Argue Agreeably .... page 65 ▶
Teens play a letter-guessing game using sentences that suggest ways to argue agreeably. Teens realize that well-communicated disagreements can help them learn to negotiate fairly.

What Love Is and What Love Is Not .... page 67 ▶
Teens note that media, pop culture and some environments, promote and glorify negative aspects of romance. Teens write words or phrases for each letter of the alphabet that illustrate what love is and is not.

My Relationships with Romantic Partners

Loves Me, Loves Me Not

Label the flower petals with the number of each statement that describes a relationship that you are in now, or have been in recently. If necessary, put more than one number in a petal.

One? Both of Us?

1. Lives only for each other
2. Encourages outside interests
3. Acts possessive and jealous
4. Assumes the role of the leader or the follower
5. Tries to change the other
6. Has own friends as well as the same friends
7. Needs constant contact
8. Feels obsessed with the other's approval
9. Is able to enjoy time away from the other
10. Can't be happy without the other nearby
11. Supports the other in bad and good times
12. Avoids power struggles
13. Respects boundaries
14. Takes turns choosing activities
15. Will only spend time with one's own friends
16. Tells the other "No one else would have you."
17. Feels comfortable to speak freely about anything
18. Brings out the worst in the other
19. Brings out the best in the other
20. Needs to save the other
21. Sees the other as perfect
22. Allows no emotional, verbal, sexual, physical or financial abuse
23. Acts with honesty and trust
24. Keeps own identity
25. Has fear of abandonment
26. Denies unpleasant facts about the other

TEENS – Relationships with People, Places and Things

Loves Me, Loves Me Not
FOR THE FACILITATOR

I. Purpose
To examine the aspects of one's romantic relationships; differentiate between healthy and unhealthy relationships.

II. General Comments
Teens sometimes are enmeshed in lopsided, smothering, obsessive or abusive romances.

III. Possible Activities
   a. If possible display a flower or photo of a daisy.
   b. Write "Loves Me, Loves Me Not" on the board and ask if anyone has played this game.
   c. If teens are unfamiliar, explain that people say, "Loves me, Loves me not," alternately as they pick petals off a flower; the phrase they say when they remove the last flower is supposed to be the truth.
   d. Explain teens will play a version of the game to heighten their understanding of their own relationships.
   e. Distribute the *Loves Me, Loves Me Not* handout; a volunteer reads the directions aloud.
   f. Allow time for completion.
   g. Encourage teens to share their responses.
   h. Ask which numbers that indicate a healthy love relationship: 2, 6, 9, 11, 12, 13, 14, 17, 19, 22, 23, 24.
   i. Encourage teens to identify why the other letters indicate unhealthy relationships.
   Possibilities
   1. Contentment with life, friendships and time with family is not dependent on the relationship.
   3. No one *owns* a partner; secure people do not get upset if they see their partner talking to someone.
   4. Equals take turns leading and following depending on situations; one doesn't control the other.
   5. Rarely can one person change the other; they accept each other's individual differences.
   7. Constant face-to-face or technological contact does not allow partners to pursue separate activities or to be their own person.
   8. Approval from a loved one feels good; equally important is to feel good about oneself and to be true to oneself.
   10. To prefer to be together is understandable, but to be desperate and obsessed is not healthy.
   15. Healthy couples take turns being with each other's friends and family.
   16. Abusers tell partners no one else would love them to prevent the partners from leaving.
   18. Healthy partners look for the best in each other and don't *push buttons* that bring out the worst.
   20. To try to save someone suggests codependency; partners help themselves and each other.
   21. No one is perfect; healthy couples are aware of each other's positive and negative actions.
   25. Fear of abandonment results in clinging to an abusive partner or destructive relationship.
   26. Partners need to see the truth, even if it means a break-up.

IV. Enrichment Activities
   a. Encourage teens to brainstorm song lyrics that suggest unhealthy relationships.
   b. Ask teens to identify attributes that lead to positive relationships.
   Possibilities
   - High self esteem (upholds one's own beliefs and values).
   - Self-preservation awareness (protects oneself from harm; maintains own identity).
   - Educational and career goals (the romance is not the only important thing in one's life).
   - Supportive friends and family (the partner is not the only important person in one's life).
   - Wisdom (to know when to work it out and when to walk away).

My Relationships with Romantic Partners

BitterSweet Dating Violence

1. Describe each stage in the cycle of dating violence on the lines provided.

1. Tension Building
_____
_____
_____
_____
_____

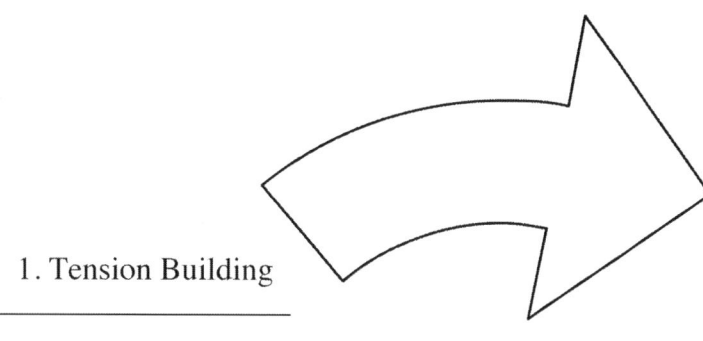

2. Abusive Incident
_____
_____
_____
_____
_____

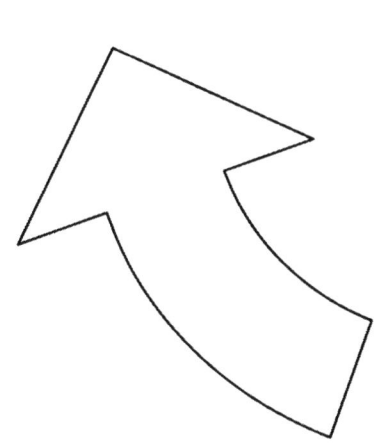

3. Honeymoon Period
_____
_____
_____
_____
_____
_____

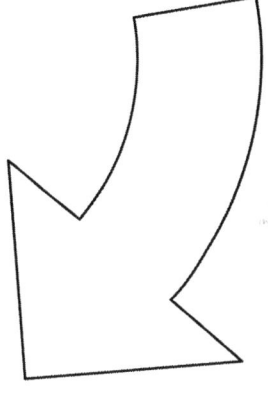

2. What numbers represent the bitter parts of the romance? _____

3. Which number is dripping with sweetness? _____

4. Is the gain worth the pain? _____

5. Explain

_____
_____

© 2014 WHOLE PERSON ASSOCIATES, 101 W. 2ND ST., SUITE 203, DULUTH MN 55802 • 800-247-6789

TEENS – Relationships with People, Places and Things

BitterSweet Dating Violence
FOR THE FACILITATOR

I. Purpose
To recognize the cycle of dating/domestic violence; to stop the abuse and/or leave the relationship.

II. General Comments
Teens who can recognize the types and signs of abuse, are better able to prevent victimization and/or seek help.

III. Possible Activities
   a. Write "BitterSweet" on the board and ask its meaning (tasting both bitter and sweet).
   b. Ask how *bittersweet* relates to some relationships (sadness and happiness all at the same time).
   c. Explain that abusive romances seem loving and exciting yet cause emotional and physical damage.
   d. Introduce teens to different types of abuse through the team or group format.
   Team Format
   - Assign 4 teams: *Control; Verbal and Emotional Abuse; Physical Abuse; Sexual Abuse.*
   - Each team brainstorms examples of their assigned type of abuse as a secretary documents.
   - The group re-convenes and secretaries share their teams' responses.
   Group Format
   - Write the types of abuse on the board.
   - Teens brainstorm behaviors indicative of each type of abuse; volunteers list ideas on the board.
   Examples
   - *Control* – monitors partner's activities, prevents partner from seeing friends and pursuing interests, dictates what to wear, plans outings, disregards partner's feelings, discourages ambitions.
   - *Verbal and Emotional Abuse* – threatens to tell secrets if partner doesn't comply with demands, resorts to name-calling and put-downs, threatens to harm partner, self or others.
   - *Physical Abuse* – hits, punches, pulls hair, spits, grabs, kicks, strangles, has a weapon.
   - *Sexual Abuse* – unwanted touching, kissing and sex, refuses to practice safe sex.
   e. Distribute the *BitterSweet Dating Violence* handout.
   f. Teens will consider a current or past romance if applicable, or imagine how the cycle could occur.
   g. Allow time for completion; encourage teens to share their responses.
   Possibilities
   1. Descriptions:
      - Tension Building – Abuser experiences mounting anger, jealousy, and etc.; victim may deny warning signs, give in to demands (to keep peace); neither communicates real concerns.
      - Abusive Incident – Abuser lashes out then blames the victim for "making me do it"; victim feels helpless, ashamed, and may feel guilty and blame self.
      - Honeymoon Period – Abuser apologizes, promises to change, may romance the victim with loving words and gifts; victim has mixed feelings, may minimize the danger and destruction.
   2. Numbers 1 and 2, Tension Building and Abusive Incident are bitter.
   3. Number 3, Honeymoon Period, drips with short-lived sweetness.
   4. Some may say gain outweighs pain; elicit that the honeymoon is not worth the pain.
   5. The pain leaves invisible and possibly visible scars; abuse tends to worsen and may lead to death.
   h. Explain that partners who abuse and victims can be helped; tell a trusted adult or seek counseling.
   i. Advise if danger is imminent, to leave the situation and/or call 911 or their local emergency number.
   j. Ask teens to discuss how the cycle can be broken at any phase (relieve tension through communication, leave the abusive situation, don't believe the false promises whispered during the honeymoon stage).

IV. Enrichment Activities
Encourage a discussion of signs that a friend is being abused (suspicious injuries, etc.)

My Relationships with Romantic Partners

Costs and Benefits

Analyze your past and current relationships' costs and benefits.

PAST RELATIONSHIP(S)

Partner's Name Code	What I Gave Up (Costs)	What I Received (Benefits)	Were the Benefits Worth the Cost?
Example: ABM	My safety – I was abused. My credibility – I hid bruises and lied.	False hopes when every time I was told it would never happen again.	No
Example: DAW	I couldn't always have my own way.	I learned about compromising.	Yes

CURRENT RELATIONSHIP(S)

Partner's Name Code	What I Give Up (Costs)	What I Receive (Benefits)	Are the Benefits Worth the Cost?
Example: EMP	My self-respect – My partner insults me.	The security to know that I have a Saturday night date.	No
Example: DJR	The attention and excitement of flirting and dating a lot of people.	A relationship based on mutual love and trust.	Yes

© 2014 WHOLE PERSON ASSOCIATES, 101 W. 2ND ST., SUITE 203, DULUTH MN 55802 • 800-247-6789

TEENS – Relationships with People, Places and Things

Costs and Benefits
FOR THE FACILITATOR

I. Purpose
To evaluate the emotional, physical, social, financial, intellectual, sexual or other costs of a relationship.

II. General Comments
Teens may pay an exorbitant price for an unhealthy romance or a fair price for a valuable relationship.

III. Possible Activities
   a. Recruit a volunteer to display a recent purchase (cell phone, jewelry, shoes, etc.).
   b. Ask the person "What did you consider before you bought the item?" (the features, price, etc.).
   c. Pose the question "What do you consider when you're in a romance?" (personalized answers).
   d. Ask "In economics and in relationships why weigh the costs and benefits?" (to determine the value).
   e. Distribute the *Costs and Benefits* handout; a volunteer reads the directions and examples aloud.
   f. Allow time for completion.
   g. Encourage teens to share their responses and receive peer feedback.
   h. Ask teens to define relationship costs that are too high under any circumstances.
   Possibilities
   - Humiliation, loss of self-respect, compromising beliefs or values
   - Risk of life and safety by being with someone who drinks/drug-uses/texts, and then drives
   - Get in trouble by being with someone who engages in illegal activities
   - Give up college or career opportunities for someone who has no goals
   - Emotional, physical, sexual, verbal bullying and/or abuse
   - Requires secrecy and/or dishonesty
   - Lose own individuality
   - Bring out the worst in each other
   - Need to hide the relationship

IV. Enrichment Activities
Copy the following table and bold text and onto the board; teens take turns filling in the blanks.
Possibilities are italicized.

ASPECTS OF RELATIONSHIPS	COSTS	BENEFITS
Emotional - Unhealthy	*Worry if it's on-again-off-again*	*Excitement in the moment*
Emotional - Healthy	*The risk of loving someone*	*Receiving love*
Physical - Unhealthy	*Perfect body to please partner*	*Being desired*
Physical - Healthy	*Energy to exercise together*	*Fitness for both partners*
Social - Unhealthy	*Give up one's own friends*	*More time with partner?*
Social - Healthy	*Time spent with partner's family*	*Learn about their culture*
Financial - Unhealthy	*Spend too much money on partner*	*Affection?*
Financial - Healthy	*Spend moderately on each other*	*Learn to love on a budget*
Intellectual - Unhealthy	*Give up one's own interests*	*Please partner?*
Intellectual - Healthy	*Work hard toward goals*	*Self-development for both*
Sexual - Unhealthy	*Pushed into unwanted activities*	*Keep the partner?*
Sexual - Healthy	*Ability to say "No" and/or engage in safe sex*	*Respect each other's boundaries*

My Relationships with Romantic Partners

Amusement Park Analogies

**Depict and describe the amusement park ride(s) your dating relationship resembles.
You may draw one large amusement park ride or a collage of amusement park rides
that show different aspects of your romance.
If you have not dated, illustrate your own expectations.
You may want to show a relationship you have observed at home, a friend's home, etc.
Feel free to use symbols and cartoons, and to add labels or descriptions.**

TEENS – Relationships with People, Places and Things

Amusement Park Analogies
FOR THE FACILITATOR

I. Purpose
To express thoughts and feelings about dating relationships by comparing them to amusement park rides.

II. General Comments
Anticipation, unexpected twists and turns, peaks, whirls and free falls, etc., relate to rides and romance.

III. Possible Activities
  a. If possible procure crayons, markers, poster paper, etc.; otherwise teens use pencils and the handout.
  b. Write "Amusement Ride Bee" on the board; explain that players name rides instead of spelling words.
  c. Invite teens to stand up at their seats or in a circle.
  d. Teens take turns naming amusement park rides; people sit as they are unable to name one.
  e. Ask how dating relationships resemble amusement park rides (ups and downs, dizzying emotions).
  f. Distribute the *Amusement Park Analogies* handout; a volunteer reads the directions aloud.
  g. Emphasize that artistic ability, grammar and spelling are not important; simply imagine!
  h. Allow time for completion.
  i. Encourage teens to share their drawings and descriptions and to receive peer feedback.
  Possibilities
   - Roller Coaster – peaks and crashes, one's world may turn upside down
   - Ferris Wheel – gentle highs and lows with views to enjoy
   - Bumper Cars – frequent head butts
   - Carousel – going around in circles and getting nowhere, or a pleasant experience
   - Pendulum rides – back and forth, on and off, affection and anger
   - Scrambler or Twist – spinning out of control physically or emotionally
   - Dark rides (tunnels, haunted houses) – scary, possibly dangerous
   - Fun House – illusions (mirrors that distort), may see partner through rose colored glasses
   - Drop Towers – frightening free falls, butterflies in stomach anticipating good or bad events
   - Water Slides – into warm (nurturing) or shockingly cold (cruel) water.
   - Monorail – see the whole picture from a higher (enlightened) perspective

IV. Enrichment Activities
  a. Ask teens what keeps them safe on rides (restraints – lap bars, seat belts, harnesses, etc.).
  b. Encourage teens to ask themselves, *What keeps me emotionally and physically safe in relationships?*
  Possibilities
   - Boundaries, sticking to decisions about what they will not tolerate or engage in
   - Awareness regarding what is healthy or detrimental
   - A support system outside the relationship to help them explore feelings and issues
  c. Prompt teens to brainstorm the benefits of positive dating relationships.
  Possibilities
   - Learn to regulate strong emotions
   - Experience emotional intimacy
   - Develop one's identity as an equal partner
   - Enhance communication and conflict resolution skills
   - Love and be loved

My Relationships with Romantic Partners ▶

Does Break Up = Broken Heart?

Your thoughts about your break up can make or break you!

Example:

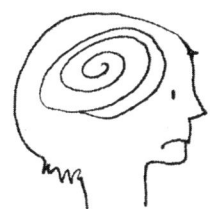

My negative thought: "I'll never get over it."

My broken-hearted feelings: sad and hopeless.

My light bulb moment of truth: "I'll feel the grief now, but I will heal."

My negative thought is …
_____

My broken hearted feeling is …
_____

My light bulb moment of truth is …
_____

> *'Tis better to have loved and lost than never to have loved at all.*
> ~ ALFRED LORD TENNYSON

How does this quote apply to you?
_____
_____

How does this quote apply to other aspects of life, not just relationships?
_____
_____

TEENS – Relationships with People, Places and Things

Does Break Up = Broken Heart?
FOR THE FACILITATOR

I. Purpose
To promote cognitive change when teens think negatively about a break up.

II. General Comments
A relationship's end can seem devastating; teens will learn they can emerge stronger and wiser.

III. Possible Activities
a. Write, "Breaking up is ..." on the board and ask teens to finish the sentence (hard to do, etc.).
b. Ask about some reasons teens break up (partner cheats, abuse, an unequal balance of power or love).
c. Encourage teens to share feelings after a break up (loss of one's role as part of a couple; sadness).
d. Distribute the *Does Break Up = Broken Heart?* handout; a volunteer reads the examples aloud.
e. If some teens never experienced a break-up ask them to write how they imagine they would think.
f. Allow time for completion.
g. Encourage teens to share their responses and receive peer feedback.

Possibilities

Negative Thoughts	Broken-Hearted Feelings	Light Bulb Truth
I'll never love again.	Empty	I will love again.
No one else will ever want me.	Lonely	I have worthwhile qualities.
This should have lasted forever.	Devastated	Many teen relationships end.
I deserved degrading treatment.	Worthless	I deserve respect.
I was victimized.	Self-pity	I am a survivor.
I was a fool to fall for my partner.	Foolish	I now know what I do and don't want.
I keep asking what went wrong.	Obsessive	I learned from the experience.

Responses will be personalized regarding the Tennyson quote.

Concepts to elicit
- To love is a risk
- Resilience results when teens survive rejection, grief, loss
- In love and life pain happens but so does joy

h. Prompt teens to identify signs that they or a friend needs additional help with their situation:
- Thoughts of suicide or urges to harm others
- Turning to alcohol, drugs, food binges or other addictions
- Pursuing rebound romances with anyone or everyone to avoid being alone
- Inability to concentrate at school or work
- Irritability and anger for no apparent reason
- A loss of interest in previously enjoyable activities
- Isolation from friends and family
- Loss of motivation and low energy
- Physical reactions – stomach aches, headaches, appetite or sleep changes

i. Suggest sources of support including parents/caregivers, counselors, spiritual advisors, therapists
j. Emphasize the importance of telling a trusted adult and/or calling 911 or their local emergency number or going to the closest hospital's Emergency Department if harm to self or others may occur.

IV. Enrichment Activities
Ask teens to brainstorm ways to handle a break up:
- Release the pain – talk to a trusted adult, journal, cry.
- Be creative – become involved and learn something brand new.
- Focus on others – initiate a fund-raiser, volunteer for a charity, advocate for a worthy cause, pursue a passion.

My Relationships with Romantic Partners ▶

Leave Respectfully

**Circle the number in front of the respectful ways to end a dating relationship.
Place an X through the numbers of the disrespectful ways to end a dating relationship.**

1. Tell everyone else first.
2. Cheat.
3. Text "I'm breaking up."
4. Talk face-to-face.
5. Criticize your partner.
6. Say, "We have different goals and needs."
7. Say, " I am not ready for an exclusive relationship."
8. Say, "I might change my mind later."
9. Say, "The relationship is just not working for me."
10. Say, "Nothing is wrong. I've just been busy lately."
11. Just stop calling or emailing.
12. Break up in front of people.
13. Talk to others about the personal aspects of your relationship.
14. Gossip about your partner's family.
15. Think about the pros and cons of the relationship before you decide.
16. Mention the person's positive qualities.
17. After the break up, continually contact the person.
18. Spread secrets.
19. Ask your best friend to break it to your partner gently.
20. Say you'll call and then, don't.

Personal opinion question – any response is right if it works for you:

Do you prefer a clean break and no further contact, or to remain friends?_____

Explain _____
_____
_____

The way you leave a relationship tells a lot about you, and whether people will respect you, and whether you'll respect yourself in that moment and in the future.

TEENS – Relationships with People, Places and Things

Leave Respectfully

FOR THE FACILITATOR

I. Purpose
To differentiate between respectful and disrespectful ways to initiate a break up.

II. General Comments
Truth and tact help teens end relationships with dignity.

III. Possible Activities
   a. Explain that teens will take a quiz for fun that does not count for a grade; it will be self-scored.
   b. Distribute the *Leave Respectfully* handout; a volunteer reads the directions aloud.
   c. Allow time for completion.
   d. Encourage teens to share their responses and rationales.
   Answer Key
   Circled numbers – 4, 6, 7, 9, 15, 16
   Reasons other numbers are not respectful:
   1. It is disrespectful to your partner to tell others first, and embarrassing if your partner is the last to find out.
   2. The time to date someone else is after the relationship ends.
   3. Texts, emails and even verbal phone calls are cowardly.
   5. Criticism tears someone down at a time when their ego may already feel damaged.
   8. Do not give false hope.
   10. Do not lie or give excuses.
   11. To just disappear leaves the person wondering what's going on.
   12. Do not publicly humiliate your partner.
   13. What happens in the relationship stays with the partners.
   14. You wouldn't want your partner to gossip about your family.
   17. Give the person time and space to grieve, get over the break up and move forward.
   18. A secret should never be revealed (unless life and safety are in danger).
   19. You break it to your partner gently; don't turn over the responsibility
   20. It is disrespectful to make promises you won't keep.
   Personal Opinion Question responses will be individualized.

IV. Enrichment Activities
Ask teens to brainstorm how the other partner can handle the break up with self-respect.
   Elicit
   - Accept what happened.
   - Forgive partner (and self if applicable).
   - Seek support from friends, family (and professionals if necessary).
   - Do not obsess about what went wrong, but do think about what you might have done to prevent it and whether that would have gone against your values. Then, let it go.
   - If time and energy are wasted checking the person out on social media – stop being a *friend*.
   - A person who keeps looking at photos compulsively may need to delete them.
   - Don't play detective to find out about your former partner's new love.
   - Focus on moving forward with self-development (school, extracurricular activities, goals).
   - Know that loving and being loved will happen again, probably in a healthier way.
   - Tell a trusted adult or call 911 or go to the closest hospital if harm to self or others is imminent.

My Relationships with Romantic Partners

Romantic Jealousy: The Other Side of the Coin

Next to the front side of the coin, write the most valuable gift the relationship gives you.

_____
_____
_____
_____

Next to the flip side of the coin, write what you fear losing.

_____
_____
_____
_____

How do your coins illustrate the Francois de La Rochefoucald quote?

Jealousy contains more of self-love than of love.

_____
_____

Consider the wisdom of Paul Eldridge:

Jealousy would be far less torturous if we understood that love is a passion entirely unrelated to our merits.

What is meant by "... love is a passion"?

_____

Why can we be more secure when our partner's love for us is not related to only our good points?

_____
_____

How does the quote help remove the sting if our partner prefers someone else?

_____
_____

TEENS – Relationships with People, Places and Things

Romantic Jealousy: The Other Side of the Coin
FOR THE FACILITATOR

I. Purpose
To understand that irrational or unwarranted romantic jealousy is related to one's own insecurities.
To understand the complex nature of attraction that cannot be forced or earned.

II. General Comments
Teens fiercely guard romances that seem to meet their needs for security, love and belonging, esteem, etc.

III. Possible Activities
   a. Write "Romantic jealousy" on the board and ask its meaning (reaction to a real or imagined threat to a relationship).
   b. Ask teens to share their experiences with romantic jealousy within their comfort zones.
   c. Distribute the *Romantic Jealousy: The Other Side of the Coin* handout.
   d. Allow time for completion.
   e. Encourage teens to share their responses and receive peer feedback.
   Possibilities
   - The most valuable gift: being adored, paid attention to, listened to, part of a couple, etc.
   - The most painful fear: abandonment, humiliation if partner cheats, damaged esteem, etc.
   - The coins illustrate the quote because jealousy is all about *us* – what *we* will lose or feel.
   - A passion means an unexplainable attraction to a person even if others seem more appealing.
   - We can be secure because we won't try to force or earn our partner's love.
   - It helps remove the sting because if our partner chooses someone else it is not because they have more value and we have less; it is due to a passion that is beyond our control.

IV. Enrichment Activities
   a. Ask individuals, teams or the group to brainstorm tips to counteract jealousy.
   b. Individuals or teams share their findings or a volunteer lists the group's ideas on the board.
   Possibilities
   - Interrogation and spying will not make a cheater faithful.
   - Distrust may make a faithful partner stray.
   - Decide that one would not want to be with a partner who prefers someone else.
   - Develop one's own identity rather than focusing on one's role as part of a couple.
   - Realize there are no assurances that romantic relationships will last.
   - Enjoy the time spent regardless of whether or not the relationship will last forever.
   - Acknowledge that the end of a romance is not the end of the world.
   - Know that a person who tries to make a partner jealous confuses love with possessiveness.
   - Discuss what both partners are comfortable with regarding social media:
      Is it ok to share aspects of the relationship online?
      Is it ok to connect with an ex?
      Is it ok to be friends with flirty people?
      Do photos of prior partners cause discomfort?
   - Don't do anything in cyberspace one would not want a partner or the world to see.

My Relationships with Romantic Partners

Argue Agreeably

Plan the right time and place.

Do not let things build up and then explode.

Use "I feel" statements.

Do not push sensitive buttons.

Avoid unrelated issues from the past.

No name calling or teasing.

Make eye contact and listen.

Do not say "You always" or "You never."

Forgive and ask for forgiveness.

Hold hands if not extremely angry.

Work for win-win for the relationship.

Be open to your partner's needs and wants.

TEENS – Relationships with People, Places and Things

Argue Agreeably
FOR THE FACILITATOR

I. Purpose
To consider some fair disagreement concepts.

II. General Comments
Disagreements can be learning experiences to be able to negotiate fairly and respectfully.

III. Possible Activities
a. Before session photocopy the *Argue Agreeably* handout and cut out the sentence boxes.
b. Place cutouts face down at the front of the room.
c. Explain that teens will play a version of *Hangman* without the hanging.
d. Ask a volunteer to draw two stick figures facing each other on the board.
e. Tell teens "This represents two partners arguing."
f. Write "Game Topic: Argue Agreeably" on the board.
g. Explain that when it is their turn each player will:
   - Draw two stick figures on the board.
   - Pick up a cutout that contains a sentence about arguing agreeably.
   - Copy the blank lines for each letter and the spaces between words onto the board.
   - Call on players who take turns guessing letters.
   - Write the correctly guessed letters on the blanks.
   - Write incorrectly guessed letters off to the side.
   - Erase a stick figure's body part for each incorrectly guessed letter.
   - If all parts of both stick figures are erased, fill in all blanks to reveal the sentence.
h. Tell teens that a player wins by correctly guessing all words in the sentence.
i. A winner gives a brief example or personal story about the concept, then takes a turn at the board.

IV. Enrichment Activities
a. Give teens slips of paper on which to write their own sentences.
b. Ask teens to select a topic.
   Possibilities
   - Ways to show you care for your partner.
   - What it means to "agree to disagree."
c. Teens take turns at the board, writing blanks for the letters in their sentences.
d. Peers guess letters and the game proceeds as in III above.

My Relationships with Romantic Partners

What Love Is and What Love Is Not

What Love Is

Starting with each letter, write a word, phrase, image or symbol, that describes **what love is**.

A	N
B	O
C	P
D	Q
E	R
F	S
G	T
H	U
I	V
J	W
K	X
L	Y
M	Z

- -

What Love Is Not

Starting with each letter, write a word, phrase, image or symbol, that describes **what love is not**.

A	N
B	O
C	P
D	Q
E	R
F	S
G	T
H	U
I	V
J	W
K	X
L	Y
M	Z

TEENS – Relationships with People, Places and Things

What Love Is and What Love Is Not
FOR THE FACILITATOR

I. Purpose
To differentiate between a healthy love relationship and one that is not.

II. General Comments
The media, pop culture and some teens' environments often portray negative aspects of romance.

III. Possible Activities
a. Before session photocopy and cut one handout for teams or make enough copies for each individual.
b. Pose the question "How do you know you are in love?" (accept individualized responses).

Team Format
- One team receives the *What Love Is* list and the other team receives *What Love Is Not*.
- Each team elects a secretary to list their ideas on the page. Allow time for completion.
- The group re-convenes; secretaries share their teams' responses and receive peer feedback.

Individual Format
- Distribute the *What Love Is and What Love Is Not* handout to each teen; a volunteer reads the directions aloud.
- Allow time for completion. Encourage teens to share their responses and receive peer feedback.

Board Activity Format:
- Copy the handout on the board – the alphabet and headings *What Love Is* and *What Love Is Not*.
- Teens take turns writing words or phrases that start with each letter under each phrase above.

Possibilities for What Love Is

Affection, Appreciation, Acceptance	Nurturing, Nice
Build up, Balance	Openness
Commitment, Communication, Compromise, Care	Pleasure, Passion, Patience, Protection
Dependable	Questions and answers
Excitement, Empathy, Encouragement, Equality	Responsibility, Respecting differences, Romance
Friendship, Forgiveness, Faith	Sharing, Strong feelings, Support
Generosity, Give-and-take	Trust, Tolerance
Hard work, Honesty	Understanding
Individuality, Interaction	Vulnerability, Value
Joy, Joyful attitude	Warmth, Wonderful
Kindness	X and O (Symbols for Kiss and Hug)
Loyalty	Young and old
Maturity, Mutual caring	Zeal

Possibilities for What Love Is Not

Abuse (physical, emotional, verbal, sexual)	Negative Comments, Name Calling, Neglect
Bullying, Badmouthing, Blaming	Obsession
Cruelty, Clinginess, Control, Competition	Possessiveness, Pain, Proving One's Self, Power
Dependency, Disrespect, Demanding, Demeaning	Questioning Fidelity, Quick Fix
Expecting all needs to be met, Envy	Rose Colored Glasses, Resentment, Rudeness
Fear, Force	Selfishness, Sneaky, Sexual Pressure, Stalking
Giving up own identity, Grudges	Temper Tantrums
Humiliation, Hurt	Unsafe Sex, Unkindness
Intimidation, Insecurity, Infatuation, Infidelity	Violence, Vindictiveness
Jealousy	Wandering, Wondering, Worrying
Kiss and Tell	X-Rated Photos
Lies, Lust only	Yelling, Yammering
Manipulation, Mistrust, Mixed Messages	Zoning-Out

IV. Enrichment Activities
Encourage teens to identify which word or phrase is most meaningful to them and to elaborate.

MY RELATIONSHIPS WITH PLACES

> *Blessed are they who see beautiful things in humble places where other people see nothing.*
> ~ Camille Pissarro

My Most Memorable Childhood Home .... page 71 ▶
Teens recall the place, people and culture that most affected them in either a positive way or a negative way. Teens define "broken home" and how it can be repaired, and decide what makes a house a home.

Location, Location, Location .... page 73 ▶
Teens identify places that most likely foster optimal development or have probable detrimental effects. Teens brainstorm places where they can meet their needs, e.g., love, self-development, social life, etc.

People at My School .... page 75 ▶
Teens learn that all kinds of people are everywhere; whom they choose to focus on makes the difference. Teens work toward solutions at their school rather than dwelling on problems.

Place of Mind .... page 77 ▶
Teens practice thought stopping and reframing as they zoom from "Don't Go There" to "Go There." Teens learn to acquire peace of mind through relaxation techniques, and by helping others in need.

My Relationships with Places ▶

My Most Memorable Childhood Home

Write a few words about the home in which you have the most positive and/or negative memories.

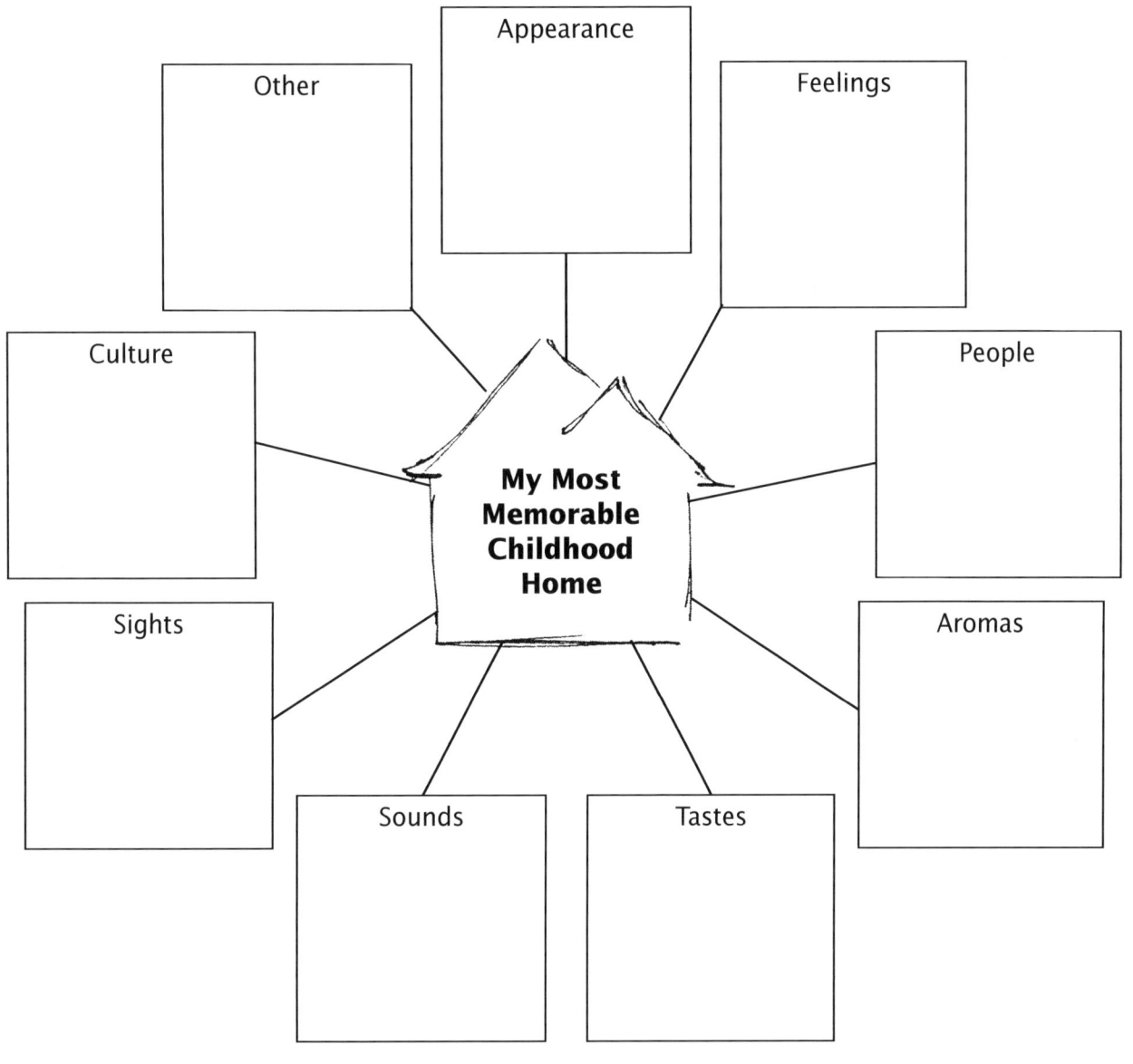

How did you feel about this home during your childhood?
_____
_____
_____

Look back. From your more mature perspective, how has that home affected you?
_____
_____
_____

TEENS – Relationships with People, Places and Things

My Most Memorable Childhood Home

FOR THE FACILITATOR

I. Purpose
To focus on the place that most affected one's formative years.

II. General Comments
Some teens may have moved frequently; in this session they choose their most meaningful home.

III. Possible Activities
  a. Recruit a volunteer to draw a house on the board.
  b. Ask teens about different types of homes (apartments, a relative's place, foster or group homes, etc.).
  c. Request a show of hands: "Who has lived in only one place?" "Who has moved at least three times?"
  d. Distribute the *My Most Memorable Childhood Home* handout.
  e. Emphasize that teens will focus on the home with the most positive and/or negative memories.
  f. Prompt teens to consider both helpful and hurtful aspects of the home.
  g. Allow time for completion.
  h. Encourage teens to share their responses and receive peer feedback.

  Possibilities
  - Appearance – neat, neglected, *lived-in*, too perfect, fancy, functional, new, old
  - Feelings – safe, secure, afraid, nurtured, ignored, loved, criticized, encouraged, warm, cold
  - People – supportive, constant conflict, addictive, strict, lenient, role models, abusive
  - Aromas – cleaning products, food being cooked, bath soaps, colognes, pet odors, body odors, dirt
  - Tastes – foods associated with comfort, holidays, rewards, disliked, being forced
  - Sounds – music, conversation, arguments, cursing, praying, laughter, crying, put-downs, compliments
  - Sights – hand-holding, kissing, hugging, physical, verbal, emotional and/or sexual violence, tools, hobby supplies, bullying
  - Culture – having or lacking religious symbols, art, music, books, computers
  - Other – individualized responses (drugs, alcohol, weapons, gardens, isolation, secrets, poverty, lack of food, gas, electricity, welcoming visitors, celebrations, etc.)

IV. Enrichment Activities
Ask teens to define the expression *broken home* (split apart by divorce or separation).
  a. Share another meaning of *broken* – (destroyed or badly affected by misfortune or grief).
  b. Ask for other examples of homes that are *broken* (troubled by abuse and/or addiction).
  c. Ask teens to brainstorm how a *broken home* can be repaired.

  Possibilities
  - If due to caregiver separation, both homes can provide love.
  - If due to abuse, the abuser or the victims can be removed and/or assisted with counseling.
  - If due to addiction, the addict or alcoholic and the family can receive treatment.
  - Secrets can be revealed to a trusted adult.
  - Social service agencies can assist with food, utilities, housing, clothing, education, employment, etc.

  d. Pose the question "What makes a house a home?" (responses will vary).

  Elicit
  - Money, furnishings; a fancy car, big boat or recreational vehicle in the driveway ***do not***.
  - Love, trust, communication, respect, conflict resolution, faith, ***do*** make a house a home.

My Relationships with Places ▶

Location, Location, Location

Write, draw, sketch or use icons to show ALL of the places in your life
(school, home, restaurant, place of worship, friends, hang-out, etc.) on the game board below.
You may arrange the places in any way – scattered in a collage, along a path, around the border, etc.

```
┌─────────────────────────────────────────┐
│              LOCATIONS                  │
│                                         │
│                                         │
│                                         │
│                                         │
│                                         │
│                                         │
│                                         │
│                                         │
└─────────────────────────────────────────┘
```

Many places in your life may have both positive potential influences and negative potential influences on your attitudes and behaviors.

- Place a plus sign (+) next to places most likely to have more of a positive influence on you than negative.
- Place a minus sign (-) next to places most likely to have more of a negative influence on you than positive.
- Place a question mark (?) next to places you are wondering about.

TEENS – Relationships with People, Places and Things

Location, Location, Location

FOR THE FACILITATOR

I. Purpose
To identify places most likely to foster optimal development and those with probable detrimental effects.

II. General Comments
Many places in a teen's life may have both positive potential influences and negative potential influences on their attitudes and behaviors. Teens are encouraged to choose primarily productive rather than destructive environments.

III. Possible Activities
   a. Write "Location, location, location!" on the board and ask its meaning (the #1 rule in real estate, identical homes have more or less value depending on location e.g. beach front versus busy street).
   b. Ask teens how the locations in which they place themselves affect their lives (safe or dangerous can mean life or death; places in which legal or illegal activities occur may affect their freedom etc.).
   c. Prompt teens to name games in which location matters (monopoly, etc.).
   d. Suggest that teens close their eyes and visualize the locations in their lives as on a game board.
   e. Distribute the *Location, Location, Location* handout; a volunteer reads the directions aloud.
   f. Point out that many places can be positive, negative, or both (e.g. school may be helpful for education but hurtful if bullying occurs) but most have a primarily productive or destructive potential.
   g. Tell teens not to worry about art or spelling but to comprehensively show all the places they may go.
   h. Allow time for completion.
   i. Encourage teens to share their work and receive peer feedback.

   Possibilities
   - Most likely to have a positive influence – school, workplace, house of worship, extracurricular activities, sporting events, art galleries, museums, concerts (if not promoting alcohol, drugs or violence).
   - Most likely to have a negative influence – gatherings in which alcohol, drugs, weapons or violence are present; cars in which drivers are impaired by substances or distracted by texting; places in which people exclude, gossip or bully; places in which gambling, unsafe or unwanted sex, pornography are promoted, etc.
   - Questionable places – a new friend's or new partner's house; a party with unfamiliar people; a nature walk along an unknown path; unknown websites or chat rooms, dark places at night, etc.

IV. Enrichment Activities
Ask teens to brainstorm common needs, and then places in which their needs may be met.

   Possibilities
   - Love and Belonging – home if parents/caregivers provide nurturing and guidance; possibly the homes of extended family and/or friends, etc.
   - Education – schools, libraries, museums, state parks, nature preserves, zoos, etc.
   - Social life – clubs, teams, chorus, band, scouting, 4-H, etc.
   - Spirituality – houses of worship, nature, bookstores offering inspirational literature, etc.
   - Self-development – music, art, dance, theater and other lessons; sports; contests that showcase one's writing, public speaking, debating skills; academic competitions, spelling bees, etc.
   - Emotional expression – places that offer counseling, support groups, etc.
   - Physical health – medical clinics, reputable nutrition programs, gyms, safe areas for jogging, etc.
   - Career – places that offer vocational assessments and guidance e.g. school counseling office, community college admissions departments (depending on one's age); volunteer sites to try out aspects of occupations one is considering, etc.

People at My School

A high school senior volunteered to welcome new students.

The first newcomer asked, "What kind of people are at this school?"

The greeter asked, "What kind people were at your old school?"

The newcomer said, "There were snobs, cliques and bullies."

The greeter said, "If that's who you found at your old school, that's who you might find here too."

A second newcomer asked, "What kind of people are at this school?"

The greeter asked, "What kind of people were at your old school?"

The newcomer said, "The students were friendly, people helped each other and the teachers cared."

The greeter said, "If that's who you found at your old school, that's who you might find here too."

1. Do you think snobs, cliques and bullies represented *everyone* at the first student's old school? _____

2. Do you think *friendly*, *helpful* and *caring* describes *everyone* at the second student's old school? _____

3. Why did the greeter tell the both newcomers "That's who you might find here, too"?
_____
_____
_____

4. What kind of people do you choose to find at your school?
_____
_____
_____

All kinds of people are everywhere
Whom we choose to focus on makes the difference.
Find where you fit in.

TEENS – Relationships with People, Places and Things

People at My School
FOR THE FACILITATOR

I. Purpose
To learn that one's mindset significantly influences expectations and perceptions; teens who bring old attitudes to new situations may experience the *same old* outcomes.

II. General Comments
Through a story or skit, teens will realize that all kinds of people are everywhere; whom they choose to focus on makes the difference.

III. Possible Activities
  a. Before session decide whether to use the Skit or Individual Format.
     Skit Format
     - Recruit four teens to act as narrator, greeter, first and second newcomers.
     - Give actors copies of the *People At My School* handout and allow a few minutes to rehearse.
     - The actors perform the skit and return to their seats; the audience applauds.
     - Ask teens to share their thoughts about the performance's message (individualized responses).
     - Distribute the *People At My School* handout to all teens and allow time for completion.
     - Encourage teens to share their responses.

     Individual Format
     - Distribute the *People At My School* handout; ask a volunteer to read the story aloud.
     - Allow time for completion; encourage teens to share their responses.

     Possibilities
     1. No
     2. No
     3. Newcomers who focused on negative or positive people in the past will tend to focus on the same types of people at the new school.
     4. Teens will ideally describe people with positive traits (individualized responses).

  b. Suggest that teens consider the role of their expectations on their perceptions of an overall negative or positive school social climate (whether they are looking for the worst or the best in the situation).

  c. Encourage discussion and debate about whether the greeter was right or wrong in telling both newcomers "That's who you might find here too."
     Possibilities
     - Right because newcomers will probably experience new situations in the same old ways.
     - Wrong because the greeter promoted negative expectations for the first newcomer.

  d. Ask teens what the greeter could have said.
     Possibilities
     - "There are friendly and unfriendly people everywhere; whom we choose to focus on affects our experience."
     - "Look for the best people, classes and teachers and you will probably find them."

  e. Prompt teens to identify the kind of school social climate they choose to embrace (acceptance, inclusion, respect for different cultures, open to new ideas, varied extracurricular activities, etc.).

IV. Enrichment Activities
  a. Write Abraham Lincoln's quote on the board: "He has the right to criticize who has the heart to help."
  b. Encourage teens to brainstorm ways to solve problems at their school (vs. dwelling on negativity).
  c. Responses will be individualized based on each school's unique situations.
     Examples
     - Bullying – start an anti-bullying campaign with posters, school newspaper articles, etc.
     - Limited extracurricular activities – start clubs, raise funds for programs, etc.

My Relationships with Places

Place of Mind

Your peace of mind depends on the places where you allow your mind to go.
Train your mind to *zoom* from "Don't Go There!" to "Go There."
Draw a line from each stressful thought on the left to a *stress-less* thought on the right.

Don't Go There!	Go There
1. "I wonder who my ex is dating."	A. "I will develop study skills."
2. "I won't get into the best college."	B. "I will do my best."
3. "No one wants to go out with me."	C. "My true friends accept me."
4. "A drink will soothe my nerves."	D. "Letting go is better."
5. "Stimulants help me study."	E. "I've grown beyond wondering."
6. "Everybody does it."	F. "I express myself assertively."
7. "I'll lie my way out of trouble."	G. "I can conquer my fears."
8. "I'm afraid to try out for …"	H. "I'll get help and then help myself."
9. "I wish I could look like that person."	I. "There are many excellent schools."
10. "My life won't get any better."	J. "I'll think calm thoughts."
11. "Revenge is sweet."	K. "I'll hang around like-minded people."
12. "I'll never get over my guilt."	L. "I'm not everybody."
13. "I'm never the best."	M. "Honesty is easier than remembering the lies."
14. "I expect everyone to like me."	N. "I celebrate my unique traits."
15. "I'm afraid to speak my mind."	O. "I forgive myself."

Personalize these sentences:

I will tell myself "Don't go there!" if I start to think about _____

_____

My "Go there" thought will be _____

_____

TEENS – Relationships with People, Places and Things

Place of Mind
FOR THE FACILITATOR

I. Purpose
   To use thought stopping and reframing when one's mind wanders into negative territory.

II. General Comments
   Teens will connect peace of mind with the places they allow their minds to go.

III. Possible Activities
   a. Before session recruit two volunteers to enact this scenario:
      One friend says "Guess what I heard about your ex?"
      The other friend says "Don't go there!"
   b. When session starts the actors perform the skit.
   c. Audience claps and actors return to their seats.
   d. Ask the group "Why did the friend say 'Don't go there'?" (to avoid re-kindling feelings).
   e. Invite teens to share times they have told people "Don't go there" (individualized responses).
   f. Pose the question "How many of you have told your own mind 'Don't go there'?" (show of hands).
   g. Encourage teens who raise their hands to share their situations.
   h. Distribute the *Place of Mind* handout; a volunteer reads the directions aloud.
   i. Allow time for completion; review the matching exercise.
      Answer Key:

1. E	6. L	11. D
2. I	7. M	12. O
3. K	8. G	13. B
4. J	9. N	14. C
5. A	10. H	15. F

   j. Encourage teens to share their sentences at the bottom of the page and receive peer feedback.

IV. Enrichment Activities
   a. Encourage teens to share peaceful places they have experienced (a cozy room, nature, etc.).
   b. Suggest that teens mentally re-experience their peaceful place by using their senses.
      Example
      - Use imagination to lie on the beach, feel soft sand and the sun's warmth, hear the waves, smell the water and see blue sky and fluffy clouds.
   c. Encourage teens to visualize themselves capably handling a challenge.
      Examples
      - Envision doing one's best in a competition regardless of the outcome.
      - Picture oneself speaking assertively to parents/caregivers about career goals whether or not they approve.
   d. Encourage teens to discuss ways to take one's mind off oneself and think about others.
      Example
      - Volunteer for fundraisers at school, read to children at the library, help coach a sports team.
   e. Encourage teens to practice relaxation techniques for body and mind.
      Examples
      - Breathing technique – breathe in fully through the nose ("smell the roses") and out through the mouth ("blow out the candle"). They may repeat words that work for them ("In with faith, out with fear," "In with the positive, out with negative," etc.)
      - Muscle relaxation, exercise, warm bath, pleasant fragrances, etc.

MY RELATIONSHIPS WITH TANGIBLE THINGS 5

You affect the world by what you browse.
~ Tim Berners-Lee

My Techno-Logic .... page 81 ▶
Teens benefit from the appropriate application of technology.
Teens compose texts about technology's social, emotional, educational, and other uses or abuses.

$$$ Talks (or Not) .... page 83 ▶
Teens engage in panel discussions and consider words of wisdom about money.
Teens examine priorities, charitable goals, and the value of achievements and creative efforts.

My Most Prized Possessions .... page 85 ▶
Teens link their values to what they value: status or intangible significance.
Teens respond to "You know your possessions possess you when ..."

Slices of a Career Pie .... page 87 ▶
Teens decide personal motivations for choosing a career, e.g., high pay, pressure, passion, etc.
Teens consider the value of dreaming big but also keeping their day job.

What Gets the Best of Me? My Robbers .... page 89 ▶
What Gets the Best of Me? My Susceptibilities .... page 90 ▶
What Gets the Best of Me? My Best That It Gets .... page 91 ▶
Teens note potentially addictive substances and activities, their effects and ways to stop abusing them. Teens identify their "robbers", susceptibilities, and the best that is in them that the addiction consumes.

My Relationships with Tangible Things ▶

My Techno-Logic

Use your logic (rational thought and common sense) to *text* your reply to four of the following items. (Please respond to the following together – 1 and 2, 3 and 4, 12 and 13, 14 and 15, 19 and 20).

1. In what ways does technology help you make friends? 2. Keep friends?
3. What are some advantages of technological communication? 4. Disadvantages?
5. Describe ways you can maintain privacy online.
6. How does technology help your education?
7. In what ways does or could technology interfere with your education?
8. How do online friendships affect development of in-person relationships?
9. Share your experiences with cyber-bullying.
10. In what ways do you turn to technology to avoid facing problems?
11. Share ways technology helps you solve problems.
12. How could technology help your physical health? 13. How could it hurt your physical health?
14. How could technology help your mental health? 15. How could it hurt your mental health?
16. Describe ways online support groups could affect you.
17. In what ways does technology provide your entertainment?
18. How can technology help you define your identity?
19. Share ways your online identity is factual 20. Share ways your online identity is fictional.
21. What have been your experiences with technological flirting?
22. Share situations in which your online activity could help others.
23. Give examples of times your technological gossip hurt someone.
24. Give examples of times technological gossip or rumors were spread about you.
25. Describe photos and/or other communications you regret.
26. What would your online activity convey to college admissions counselor.
27. What would your online activity convey to a prospective employer?

Item number # _____

My Text Reply:

Item number # _____

My Text Reply:

Item number # _____

My Text Reply:

Item number # _____

My Text Reply:

TEENS – Relationships with People, Places and Things

My Techno-Logic
FOR THE FACILITATOR

I. Purpose
To promote a healthy relationship with technology.

II. General Comments
Teens' use or abuse of technology is controversial; teens benefit from its appropriate application.

III. Possible Activities
   a. Ask teens their favorite way to keep in touch with friends (probably through texts and social media).
   b. Prompt teens to compare technology to any tool that can be used or misused (used for information and positive communication or misused for inappropriate websites or cyber gossip/bullying, etc.)
   c. Distribute the *My Techno-Logic* handout; volunteers read the directions and the list of topics aloud.
   d. Allow time for completion.
   e. Encourage teens to share their responses and receive peer feedback.
      Possibilities
      1. Connect instantly to people all over the world. Add friends easily on social sites.
      2. Write frequently, stay in touch with friends from one's summer camp or prior school, etc.
      3. Advantages – non-intrusive, convenient, can edit before it is sent.
      4. Disadvantages – can't be undone, can't see facial expression, body language or hear tone of voice.
      5. Turn off location tracking apps; do not reveal personal info, address, etc.
      6. Unlimited access to research any subject; can explore colleges, careers, training, etc.
      7. A distraction if texting in class or on social or gaming sites instead of doing homework.
      8. Can help stay connected; can hurt if teens totally shy away from face-to-face friendships.
      9. Teens may share times they were victims, or perpetrators, or in situations peers have experienced.
      10. Turn on technology when corrected by a caregiver; distract oneself from issues that need attention.
      11. Research any topic on trusted websites; view a variety of opinions; seek support groups.
      12. Reliable info helps.
      13. Misleading information harms. Hurtful if it delays in-person medical treatment.
      14. Reliable information about coping skills helps.
      15. Hurtful if it delays in-person therapy; being bullied or comparing oneself to media stars or peers can interfere with valuing one's own uniqueness.
      16. Teens who are discriminated against can seek others/organizations that help overcome stigmas.
      17. Listen to music, read, watch videos and TV, play games, watch sports, and do puzzles, etc.
      18. Develop an online profile; express opinions, write prose and poetry, show photos, make videos.
      19. Teens list positive attributes and accomplishments.
      20. Teens may share information and situations that are exaggerated or untrue.
      21. Individualized responses.
      22. Visit or support charitable organizations and victims of disasters; befriend excluded people.
      23. and 24. Individualized responses.
      25. Teens may share personal stories about sexually explicit texts or photos or times when they degraded someone.
      26. and 27. Interests, values, funny and friendly communication or profanity, put-downs, etc.

IV. Enrichment Activities
   a. Encourage teens to discuss whether Short Message Service (SMS) or *textese* (slang and abbreviations) impairs language skills (it may help as teens read and write more, create and respond to words, and develop unique dialects).
   b. Ask teens to share situations in which their words were misinterpreted or they misunderstood someone's message (individualized responses).

My Relationships with Tangible Things

$$$ Talks (or Not)

PANEL DISCUSSIONS

What do you think about this quotation?

*"Don't tell me where your priorities are.
Show me where you spend your money and I'll tell you what they are."*

~ James W. Frick

Where do you spend your money?

What do you think about this quotation?

"It is not the man who has too little, but the man who craves more, that is poor."

~ Seneca

Give examples of material possessions teens crave, but don't especially need.

What do you think about this quotation?

*"Money is only a tool.
It will take you wherever you wish, but it will not replace you as the driver."*

~ Ayn Rand

Where do you hope to direct your money when you are making a living?

What do you think about this quotation?

*"Money is like love; it kills slowly and painfully the one who withholds it,
and enlivens the other who turns it on his fellow man."*

~ Kahlil Gibran

When you are making money, how can you turn it on others?

What do you think about this quotation?

*"Happiness is not in the mere possession of money;
it lies in the joy of achievement, in the thrill of creative effort."*

~ Franklin D. Roosevelt

What creative efforts thrill you?

TEENS – Relationships with People, Places and Things

$$$ Talks (or Not)

FOR THE FACILITATOR

I. Purpose
To consider words of wisdom and introduce varied attitudes about money.

II. General Comments
Teens may misjudge their own and others' success by monetary wealth; advertisers promote materialism.

III. Possible Activities

Panel Discussion Format
- Before session photocopy the *$$$ Talks (or Not)* handout and cut on the broken lines.
- Place the cutouts in a stack at the front of the room.
- Arrange some chairs at the front of the room (for teens who take turns as hosts and panelists). Option – if your group is small, arrange all chairs in a circle (all teens will participate each time).
- Write "$ Talks" on the board and ask its meaning (money provides power and influence).
- Ask teens what talks louder than money (ideas, compassion for people, passion for a cause, etc.).
- Explain that teens will portray talk show hosts and panelists who discuss money-related quotes.
- Emphasize that there are no right or wrong answers; personal opinions are to be given and respected.
- A volunteer host and panelists take seats at the front of the room; audience will watch and listen. Option – if your group is small, a teen volunteers to be host; remaining teens are panelists.
- The host picks up a cutout, reads the quotation and question aloud and encourages discussion.
- If the group is large, after panelists have spoken the host requests audience opinions, responses and questions.
- The same format is repeated with each cutout.

Individual Format
- Photocopy one *$$$ Talks (or Not)* handout per participant; do not cut on the broken lines.
- Write "$$$ Talks" on the board and ask its meaning (money provides power and influence).
- Ask teens what talks louder than money (ideas, compassion for people, passion for a cause, etc.).
- Distribute the *$$$ Talks (or Not)* handout; volunteers read the quotations and questions aloud.
- Direct teens to write responses to any or all of the questions on a separate sheet of paper.
- Encourage teens to share their responses and receive peer feedback.

Possibilities (for either format)
- What do you think? (Individualized responses regarding each quotation).
- Where do you spend your money? (Individualized responses).
- Examples of possessions teens may crave – electronics, designer clothes and shoes, cars, etc.
- Destinations for their money may be short-term treats, or college, educational field trips or travel; charitable purposes – monetary donations or trips to help people in need in other parts of the country or world, etc.
- Money can be turned on *fellow man* through fundraising to help needy students and families, to contribute to causes one believes in, to attend events and/or purchase products whose proceeds support charitable organizations, education, research, etc.
- Creative efforts that thrill may be solving a problem or brainstorming options with a friend; writing, drawing, playing music, acting in a play, photographing, debating, dancing, etc.

IV. Enrichment Activities
Encourage teens to brainstorm their own words of wisdom about money; a peer lists ideas on the board.

My Relationships with Tangible Things ▶

My Most Prized Possessions

Imagine a disaster that would force you to leave your home forever.
Your family and pets have been rescued.
You have five minutes to decide what belongings to take.

Pack your 3 most prized possessions and write them on the outside of this bag.

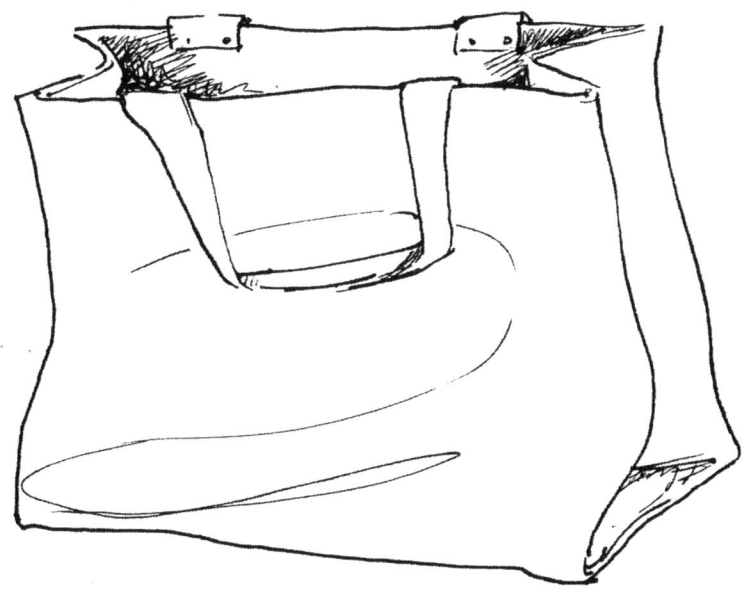

My reasons for prizing these possessions:

Item #1 _____
_____
_____

Item #2 _____
_____
_____

Item #3 _____
_____
_____

Describe a belonging that may or may not be one of the three items listed above.

Something I own that has little monetary value but means much to me is . . .

because . . .

TEENS – Relationships with People, Places and Things

My Most Prized Possessions
FOR THE FACILITATOR

I. Purpose
To consider possessions in terms of materialism and meaningfulness.

II. General Comments
Teens will be helped to *link their values* to *what they value:* status or intangible significance?

III. Possible Activities
  a. Write "Evacuate Immediately" on the board; ask when this is ordered (fire, earthquake, storms).
  b. Encourage any teens who have been evacuated from their residences to share their experiences.
  c. Distribute the *My Most Prized Possessions* handout; a volunteer reads the directions aloud.
  d. Allow time for completion; remind teens that artistic ability and perfect spelling are not required.
  e. Direct teens to look at their own *bags* and silently answer the following questions:
   - Which possessions are prized because you think they make you look good?
   - Which possessions have personal meaning and/or memories?
   - Ask teens to share their responses to the sentence completion at the bottom of the page and receive peer feedback.

IV. Enrichment Activities
  a. Ask teens to brainstorm "prized possession bags" they could provide to needy people.
  b. Recruit a volunteer to list their ideas on the board.
   Possibilities
   - Teens removed from homes by social services due to an unsafe environment: Grooming and hygiene supplies, journals, art supplies, cell phones
   - Victims of natural disasters and/or homeless people: Blankets, grooming and hygiene supplies, first aid items, non-perishable food and bottled water.
   - Elderly residents at an assisted living facility: Large print books and magazines, word-find puzzles, photo albums, hand-made greeting cards
   - Children who are hospitalized: Age-appropriate and safe toys, coloring books, art supplies, activity books and puzzles
   - Teen parents: Parenting books, diapers, skin care products for the baby, blankets, infant clothes
  c. Encourage teens to actually create and provide "prized possession bags"
   - Teens may need to organize fundraisers to purchase the items.
   - Teens may decide to approach businesses and service organizations for goods, services, funds.
  d. Write "You know your possessions possess you when you …" and encourage teens to respond.
   Possibilities
   You know your possessions possess you when you …
   - obsess about getting a bigger, better, newer version.
   - envy anyone who has a more expensive version.
   - work extra hours at the expense of study or family time to pay for your possession(s).
   - become angry when your parents don't buy you everything you want.
   - are tempted to get what you want dishonestly or illegally.
   - believe your worth depends on owning the item(s).
   - think you can't live without the item(s).
   - would never consider giving an item to someone who needs it more than you do.

My Relationships with Tangible Things ▶

Slices of a Career Pie

What matters most to you in choosing a career?

Reasons people choose careers, or add your own.

Creative Expression	Help Others	Job Readily Available	My Passion	High Pay
My Abilities	My Particular Interest(s)	Pressure from People	Prestige	Security
Other _____	Other _____	Other _____	Other _____	Other _____

**Slice the pie into different sized portions.
Label the pieces to show your career priorities.**

© 2014 WHOLE PERSON ASSOCIATES, 101 W. 2ND ST., SUITE 203, DULUTH MN 55802 • 800-247-6789

TEENS – Relationships with People, Places and Things

Slices of a Career Pie
FOR THE FACILITATOR

I. Purpose
To identify personal motivations for choosing a career.

II. General Comments
Teens may be pressured to pursue a particular career, solely seek wealth, self-actualize through work, etc.

III. Possible Activities
a. Ask teens why students work (most may say for money).
b. Question whether most teens' part-time jobs are related to their long term career goals (probably not).
c. Remind participants that as adults they may spend more than forty years working.
d. Explain that many people take the first job that comes along or are guided (or misguided) into a career.
e. Distribute the *Slices of a Career Pie* handout; a volunteer reads the directions aloud.
f. Allow time for completion.
g. Encourage teens to share their pie charts and explain reasons for their priorities.
h. Write on the board the Lao Tzu quotation:

> "Chase after money and security
> and your heart will never unclench.
>
> Care about people's approval
> and you will be their prisoner.
>
> Do your work, then stand back.
> The only path to serenity."

i. Direct teens to copy the words on the back of their handouts and save.
j. Encourage teens to analyze and personalize the poem (individualized responses).

IV. Enrichment Activities
Encourage teens to discuss and/or research related topics.
Possibilities
- How to combat *occupationism* – a form of discrimination against jobs perceived as low status which prevents some people from entering occupations in which they would find joy and success.
- How to start at the bottom rung on a career ladder – from dishwasher to chef, etc.
- How to balance work, family life, recreation, etc.
- The pros and cons of working at a disliked job because it pays well.
- The pros and cons of job satisfaction in an occupation with low pay.
- Examples of people switching careers midstream.
- The pros and cons of starting one's own business.
- Internet sources of information about occupations.
- Ways to try out occupations before beginning a course of study – volunteering, internships, etc.
- How successful people began their career paths.
- How family members chose or *fell into* their occupations.
- The value of *dreaming big* and not being discouraged by people who say "It's not realistic."
- The meaning of "Keep your day job" while dreaming big!

My Relationships with Tangible Things ▶

What Gets the Best of Me?
My Robbers

When substances and unhealthy behaviors *get the best of you* they control you and rob your time and energy.

Place a check in the box in front of items that rob you, or can rob you, if you're not careful.

ROBBERS	POTENTIAL ROBBERS IF MISUSED
❏ Alcohol	❏ Body Image Concerns
❏ Anger / Rage	❏ Food
❏ Drugs	❏ Money
❏ Gambling	❏ Risks
❏ Illegal actions	❏ Sex
❏ Lying	❏ Social Networking
❏ Obsessive love	❏ Shopping
❏ Pain (cutting, self harm)	❏ Texting
❏ Perfectionism	❏ Video Games
❏ Pornography	❏ Work
❏ Tobacco	❏ Working Out
❏ Other _____	❏ Other _____
❏ Other _____	❏ Other _____

Describe how your three biggest *robbers* control and consume you.

My Robber #1 is _____

It takes my _____

_____

My Robber #2 is _____

It takes my _____

_____

My Robber #3 is _____

It takes my _____

_____

TEENS – Relationships with People, Places and Things

What Gets the Best of Me?
My Susceptibilities

Some situations may *get the best of you* by your being more likely to use substances or engage in unhealthy behaviors.

Place a check in the boxes in front of statements that apply to you or could influence you.

MY SUSCEPTIBILITY TO THE SUBSTANCE(S) AND UNHEALTHY BEHAVIOR(S)
❑ My culture glamorizes substances and/or unhealthy behaviors. ❑ Family members turn to substances and/or unhealthy behaviors. ❑ Friends promote substances and/or unhealthy behaviors. ❑ My self-esteem is usually low. ❑ I am bored by my life. ❑ I have few or no goals. ❑ I often act before I think. ❑ I feel lonely most of the time. ❑ I struggle to fit in. ❑ I have been bullied and/or abused. ❑ I feel pressure to succeed at any cost. ❑ I have a lot of money with no specific saving or spending plans. ❑ I have not been able to receive help for possible emotional issues. ❑ I have not been able to receive help for possible physical problems. ❑ I look for the easiest way out. ❑ I have difficulty coping with anger. ❑ I have trouble facing my fears. ❑ I believe I cannot forgive myself and/or others. ❑ I struggle with feeling depressed. ❑ I feel overwhelmed by stress. ❑ Other _____ ❑ Other _____

How can you safeguard yourself from your top three susceptibilities?

My Susceptibility #1 is _____

I can safeguard myself by _____

_____

My Susceptibility #2 is _____

I can safeguard myself by _____

_____

My susceptibility #3 is _____

I can safeguard myself by _____

_____

My Relationships with Tangible Things ▶

What Gets the Best of Me? My Best That It Gets

Whatever controls and consumes you *gets the best of you* and takes the best that is *in* you.

Place a check in front of the statements that apply to you or that you are at risk of losing.

MY BEST THAT THE SUBSTANCE(S) AND UNHEALTHY BEHAVIOR(S) TAKE FROM ME
❏ My ambition runs after substances and/or unhealthy behaviors.
❏ My attention focuses on substances and/or unhealthy behaviors.
❏ My body needs more and more of substances and/or unhealthy behaviors.
❏ My energy is eaten up by substances and/or unhealthy behaviors.
❏ My existence seems to depend on substances and/or unhealthy behaviors.
❏ My family is hurt by substances and/or unhealthy behaviors.
❏ My friendships are ruined by substances and/or unhealthy behaviors.
❏ My gifts (abilities, interests, talents) are given to substances and/or unhealthy behaviors.
❏ My honesty turns to lies because of substances and/or unhealthy behaviors.
❏ My insight is blinded by denial about substances and/or unhealthy behaviors.
❏ My learning suffers because of substances and/or unhealthy behaviors.
❏ My mind is miserable without substances and/or unhealthy behaviors.
❏ My problem-solving is paralyzed by substances and/or unhealthy behaviors.
❏ My progress is stifled by substances and/or unhealthy behaviors.
❏ My relationship with substances and/or unhealthy behaviors is #1.
❏ My self-control is inadequate for substances and/or unhealthy behaviors.
❏ My self-respect has dwindled due to substances and/or unhealthy behaviors.
❏ My social life revolves around substances and/or unhealthy behaviors.
❏ My spirituality sways toward substances and/or unhealthy behaviors.
❏ My work declines due to substances and/or unhealthy behaviors.
❏ Other _____

"For all sad words of tongue and pen, the saddest are these, 'It might have been.'"

~ John Greenleaf Whittier

If you continue to be robbed of your best, someday you may say "*I* might have been" …

_____

_____

How can you reclaim the best that is in you?

a. _____

b. _____

c. _____

d. _____

TEENS – Relationships with People, Places and Things

What Gets the Best of Me?
FOR THE FACILITATOR

I. Purpose
To identify potentially addictive substances and activities; to recognize their effects; to stop abusing them.

II. General Comments
The challenges of adolescence can lead to addictive behaviors or bring out one's best.

III. Possible Activities
   a. Handouts are for three sessions; photocopy all pages. If time allows, use all three handouts for one session or use each one for three separate sessions.
   b. Distribute the *What Gets the Best of Me? My Robbers* handout, page 89.
   c. A volunteer reads the text at top of the page aloud.
   d. Allow time for completion.
   e. Encourage teens to share their responses and receive peer feedback.
   Possibilities
   - Robbers consume one's freedom, motivations, self-respect, finances, peace, health, safety, etc.
   f. Distribute the *What Gets the Best of Me? My Susceptibilities* handout, page 90.
   g. Follow steps *c, d* and *e* above.
   Possibilities
   - Teens safeguard themselves by changing their thought processes, developing goals, etc.
   h. Distribute the *What Gets the Best of Me? My Best That It Gets* handout, page 91.
   i. Follow steps *c, d* and *e* above.
   Possibilities
   - "I might have been" ambitious, energetic, healthy, a loyal friend, a caring family member, honest, insightful, a creative problem solver, spiritual, and pursuing my passion, etc.
   - Ways to reclaim one's best:
      a. Admit the problem to oneself and others.
      b. Ask for help from family, friends, professionals and support groups.
      c. Focus on the rewards of regaining the best of oneself (health, clear-mindedness, etc.).
      d. Do the work (talk, listen, read, journal, learn coping skills, change habits, etc.).
      e. Help others who have similar problems.

IV. Enrichment Activities
   a. Ask teens about pitfalls that could entice them to return to addictive substances and activities.
   Possibilities
   - Places that trigger cravings for the substance or activity.
   - People who use or abuse it.
   - Toxic people who tear down one's dreams.
   - Objects linked to it (drug paraphernalia, credit cards, photos of an unhealthy romance).
   b. Write the following word, list letters vertically, and ask teens to brainstorm what they could stand for: "BEST"
   Possibilities
   - B   Bodily health, bravery
   - E   Enthusiasm for life on life's terms
   - S   Self-love
   - T   Talents fully developed

MY RELATIONSHIPS WITH INTANGIBLE THINGS

Your most precious, valued possessions and your greatest powers are invisible and intangible. No one can take them. You, and you alone, can give them. You will receive abundance for your giving.
~ W. Clement Stone

Your time Is… .... page 95 ▶
Teens consider ways to make the most of their time and lives by reading a commencement address.
Teens compose their own speeches about time and brainstorm time management ideas.

Fortune Cookie Freedom .... page 97 ▶
Teens receive "fortunes" describing their freedoms and for each right they name a related responsibility.
Teens write affirmations for peers in fortune format and peers apply the positive messages to their lives.

Go With the Flow? .... page 99 ▶
Teens address circumstances that warrant conformity or non-conformity amidst many pressures.
Teens state when they may need a different "school of fish" that supports their aspirations and beliefs.

Expanding Ideas to Contribute to My Character .... page 101 ▶
Teens decide personal motivations for choosing a career, e.g., high pay, pressure, passion, etc.
Teens consider the value of dreaming big but also keeping their day job.

- **I Believe…** .... page 101 ▶
  Teens share beliefs and consider how what they choose to believe contributes to who they are.

- **Little Things That Are Big** .... page 102 ▶
  Teens put their spin on the topic through a blog or pictogram using drawings, symbols, etc.

- **Things That Are Broken** .... page 103 ▶
  Teens note ways to fix things within themselves and how they're "strong at the broken parts."

- **Silent Things That Are Loud** .... page 104 ▶
  Teens list what speaks loudest to them and describe a personal trait and how it is loud.

- **Things I Would Not Want to Lose** .... page 105 ▶
  Teens create posters, bumper stickers or tee shirt slogans to show what they don't want to lose.

Rivalry Rhymes .... page 107 ▶
Teens consider the pros and cons of competition and cooperation in school, sports, social life, work, etc.
Teens share their experiences and compose their own rhymes or thoughts about rivalry.

Great Moments .... page 109 ▶
Teens recognize that small acts of kindness are big.
Teens state what they would do during important endeavors when human intrusions interfere.

Ripples of Kindness .... page 111 ▶
Teens identify past, present and future ways to show compassion and learn about its personal benefits.
Teens determine how "Every act creates a ripple with no logical end."

My Relationships with Intangible Things

Your time Is…

Imagine hearing this commencement address by Steve Jobs at Stanford University.

Fill in the blanks with selections from the word bank.

| intuition thinking inner-voice become life trapped waste secondary noise courage |

"**Your time is limited, so** don't _____ it by living someone else's _____. Don't be _____ by dogma – which is living with the results of other people's _____. Don't let the _____ of others' opinions drown out your own _____ _____. **And most important** – Have the _____ to follow your heart and _____. They somehow already know what you truly want to _____. Everything else is _____."

1. Put a star in front of the line that has the most meaning for you.
2. How does it apply to you? _____
   _____
3. If you were speaking in front of your class today, what would you say?

> "Your time is _____, so…
>
>
>
> And most important…

TEENS – Relationships with People, Places and Things

Your time Is...
FOR THE FACILITATOR

I. Purpose
To consider ways to make the most of one's time and one's life.

II. General Comments
Teens may admire Steve Jobs for his contributions to technology: computers, iPods, iPads, iPhones, etc.

III. Possible Activities
  a. Explain that teens will receive an excerpt from a commencement address Steve Jobs presented on June 12, 2005 at Stanford University.
  b. Ask teens what *commencement address* means (a speech to a graduating class).
  c. Encourage teens to share info about him (entrepreneur, inventor, co-founder of Apple Inc.).
  d. Distribute the *Your Time Is...* handout; point out that the word bank will help teens fill in the blanks.
  e. Advise that the speech for number 3 can be for the present moment or as a mock graduation speech.
  f. Allow time for completion.
  g. Encourage teens to share their responses.
    Possibilities
    - Blanks: waste, life, trapped, thinking, noise, inner voice, courage, intuition, become, secondary.
    - Numbers 1-2 will be individualized responses.
    - Invite teens to give actual speeches by reading their responses to number 3 aloud.
  h. Ask teens to debate whether people always find time for what matters most to them: Some may argue that most do find time to use cell phones, play sports, or for whatever they enjoy. Others may insist there are activities they would love to do but no time due to school, work, etc.
  i. Present a riddle: "What do you do if you can't *find* time for something?" (*make* time).

IV. Enrichment Activities
  a. Encourage teens to watch the online video of Jobs' actual speech which contains additional inspiration.
  b. Ask teens to brainstorm time-management ideas as a volunteer writes them on the board. Their list can be photographed and distributed to the group or written on paper and photocopied.
    Possibilities
    - Write down all activities for a couple of days and analyze how time is spent and wasted.
    - Decide ways to increase productive pursuits and eliminate time wasters.
    - Have a planning session with oneself to decide priorities in life.
    - Plan to incorporate these priorities daily, even if for brief moments.
    - Keep a daily planner and calendar and take it everywhere (paper and pen or tech device).
    - List each day's priorities in the planner on a *Things to Do List* in order of importance.
    - Use the same planner for home, school, work, volunteer and social life; transferring data would waste time.
    - Break down large tasks into smaller steps.
    - Cross off completed items; reward oneself for finishing disliked tasks.
    - Decrease distractions – shut off cell phones and don't check email for blocks of time.
    - Use the planner to jot down ideas, or things to do for a different day as they arise.
    - Be sure to keep the planner in the same safe place at all times.
    - Understand that everything may not be completed daily; slide lower priorities over to the next day.
    - Each week review the planner entries to see trends – what does and does not get done, whether life priorities are reflected in daily priorities and how to make time for what's most important.

My Relationships with Intangible Things

Fortune Cookie Freedom

| 1 You will soon be at the wheel. | 8 Gossip is all around you. |

| 2 You may choose your friends. | 9 Education is available to you. |

| 3 A dating relationship is in your near future. | 10 Information, photos, videos and games are at your fingertips. |

| 4 You have the freedom of speech. | 11 You will soon be free to vote. |

| 5 Your brain lets you think your own thoughts. | 12 A career is around the corner. |

| 6 You want to live in a free country. | 13 You may partner with the love of your life. |

| 7 You may write and distribute your opinions. | 14 You have the right to raise a family. |

© 2014 WHOLE PERSON ASSOCIATES, 101 W. 2ND ST., SUITE 203, DULUTH MN 55802 • 800-247-6789

TEENS – Relationships with People, Places and Things

Fortune Cookie Freedom
FOR THE FACILITATOR

I. Purpose
To identify positive ways to handle freedom.

II. General Comments
Through a fortune cookie format teens think about rights and responsibilities.

III. Possible Activities
  a. Ideally, obtain enough fortune cookies to serve as snacks at the end of the session.
  b. Before session cut the *Fortune Cookie Freedom* handout on the dotted lines and fold each fortune.
  c. Place the cutouts in a container at the front of the room.
  d. When session starts ask teens to share their experiences with fortune cookies. What fortunes do they recall? Do they believe them?
  e. Explain that teens will play a game with fortunes that relate to freedom.
   - Players take turns going to the front of the room and picking up a fortune.
   - Players read the text aloud and then identify at least one related responsibility that goes along with that fortune.
   - Players may ask peers for help and peers may add to each person's idea(s).

Possibilities

Fortune Cookie Freedoms	Responsibilities
1. Driver's License	Obey rules of the road; avoid distractions, texting, drugs and alcohol.
2. Choose friends	Select people who are truthful, loyal and encouraging.
3. Date	Determine that the partner is respectful and has similar values.
4. Speak	Tell the truth, do not spread gossip, build up rather than tear down.
5. Think	*Police* own thoughts; throw out negative and replace with positive ones.
6. Free country	Obey the rules, petition for changes one believes in.
7. Write	Use judgment and caution; the world may see one's words forever!
8. Gossip	Choose what to listen to and what to repeat.
9. Education	Study seriously; pursue one's interests and maximize one's potential.
10. Media (the *press*)	Select positive and productive information and entertainment.
11. Vote	Study political and social issues; vote intelligently.
12. Career	Choose based on passions and abilities.
13. Partnership	Consider commonalities and differences and whether *love conquers all*.
14. Raise a Family	Love; learn positive parenting skills, nurture, guide, seek help as needed.

  f. Provide each teen with a few strips of paper.
  g. Ask teens to write fortunes – positive messages for peers.
  h. Teens fold and place their fortunes in a container and mix them up.
  i. Teens take turns picking up a fortune and applying it to themselves.
   Examples
   - Believe and achieve.
   - Your thoughts make you.
   - Follow your dreams.

IV. Enrichment Activities
If available, distribute fortune cookies for snacks and let teens have fun reading their fortunes aloud and ask them if they think this can come true.

My Relationships with Intangible Things

Go With the Flow?

Write and/or draw as many examples as possible for each heading.

I need to go WITH the flow ...

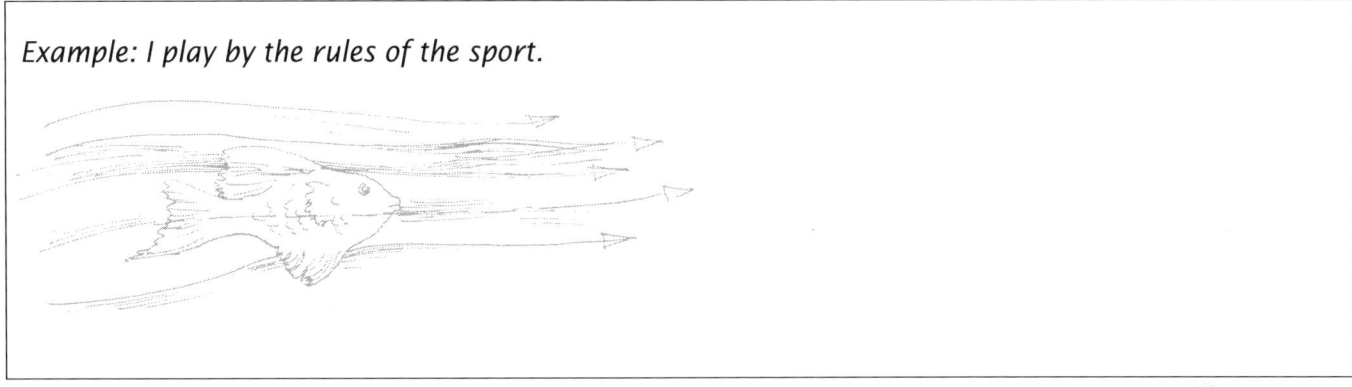

Example: I play by the rules of the sport.

I need to go AGAINST the flow ...

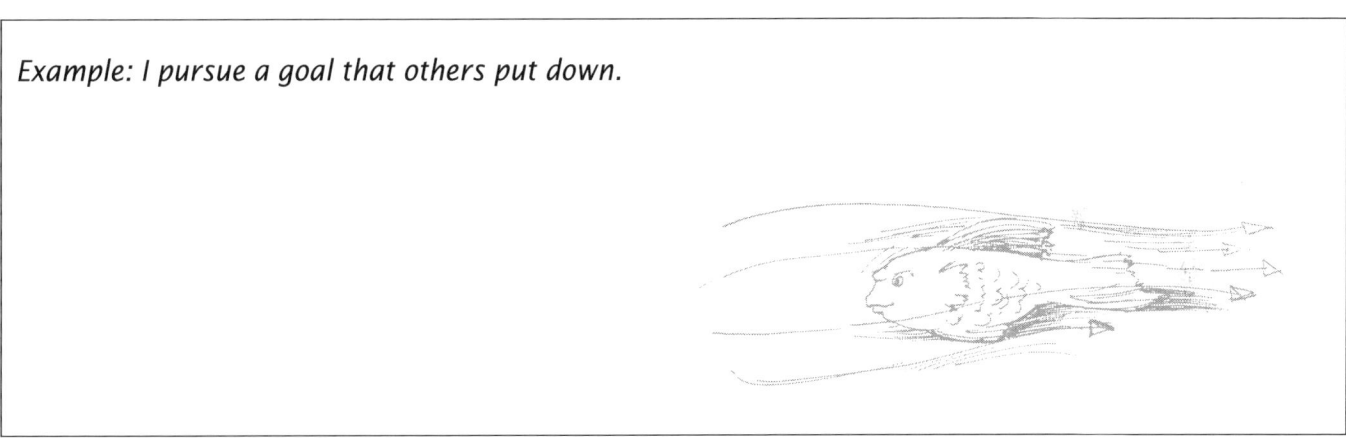

Example: I pursue a goal that others put down.

I need a DIFFERENT school of fish ...

Example: The group I'm with is dragging me down.

Go With the Flow?

FOR THE FACILITATOR

I. Purpose
To consider the circumstances that warrant conformity or non-conformity.

II. General Comments
Peers, the media, family expectations, society and subcultures exert pressure.

Teens need to decide when to conform and when to be one's own person.

III. Possible Activities
a. Ask teens what it means to "go with the flow" (comply with the trend vs. do your own thing).

b. Elicit negative, positive and neutral examples (*negative* – drink because of peer pressure; *positive* – work for good grades because it's important to my friends and me; *neutral* – follow fashion trends).

c. Write "swim against the tide" on the board and elicit its meaning (go against others' opinions).

d. Elicit negative, positive and neutral examples (*negative* – rebel against wearing a seat belt; *positive* – speak up for someone who is being bullied; *neutral* – interpret song lyrics differently than peers).

e. Pose the question "Why do fish sometimes swim upstream?" (to spawn – release eggs).

f. Ask "What can we learn from fish? (expect possible snickers or suggestive comments as teens may relate spawning to sexuality).
Elicit that we may face opposition when we pursue a goal, voice an opinion or forge a new path.

g. Ask for examples of people who swim against the current (scientists who discover and invent, composers, artists, social and political reformers, people who rise above adversity).

h. Write "School of fish" on the board and elicit that certain fish stay together and swim in the same direction, like humans who hang out together, have similar interests and goals.
Distribute the *Go With the Flow?* handout; a volunteer reads the headings and examples aloud.

i. Remind teens to think of as many personal examples as possible for each heading.

j. Allow time for completion.

k. Encourage teens to share their responses.

Possibilities
- Go with the flow to follow ...
  Rules of the road.
  Safety rules in any situation.
  Ethical considerations e.g. treat others as one wants to be treated; be non-judgmental.
  Workplace, school or home rules that cannot be negotiated.

- Go against the flow when ...
  Peers apply pressure to drink, take drugs, have unwanted or unsafe sex, cheat, lie, steal, etc.
  People practice cruelty by bullying, excluding, stereotyping, stigmatizing, fighting, etc.
  One's well thought-out opinions, values, or ambitions differ from those of friends and family.

- Find a different school of fish when ...
  Peer pressure is pulling one toward negative behavior or danger.
  A new support system is needed that promotes one's individuality, aspirations, beliefs, etc.

IV. Enrichment Activities
Encourage teens to share past experiences and the results of going with and/or against *the flow*.

My Relationships with Intangible Things

Expanding Ideas to Contribute to My Character

I Believe...

What are your top ten?

I believe ...

I believe ...

I believe ...

I believe ...

I believe ...

I believe ...

I believe ...

I believe ...

I believe ...

I believe ...

"It's what you choose to believe that makes you the person you are."
~Karen Marie Moning

Which belief contributes most to the person YOU are?

_____
_____

TEENS – Relationships with People, Places and Things

Expanding Ideas to Contribute to My Character
Little Things That Are Big…

LITTLE things can cause BIG hurts, hurdles and hassles.

LITTLE things can also show love and positive emotions in a BIG way.

**Put your spin on the topic.
Write a blog and/or create a *pictogram* (drawings, symbols, etc.) to explain …**

Little **Things That Are** *Big*

My Relationships with Intangible Things ▶

Expanding Ideas to Contribute to My Character
Things That Are Broken…

Broken has many meanings:
1. No longer whole
2. Out of order
3. Not kept
4. Not continuous
5. Uneven
6. Weakened
7. Demoralized
8. Split apart
9. Disorganized
10. Shattered

Things that are broken within me …
_____
_____

What I can do to fix them …
_____
_____

Things that are broken in my world (family, school, community, etc.) …
_____
_____

What can I do to help fix them?
_____
_____

"The world breaks everyone, and afterward, some are strong at the broken parts."
~ Ernest Hemingway

In what ways are you "strong at the broken parts"?
_____
_____

Expanding Ideas to Contribute to My Character
Silent Things That Are Loud…

What speaks loudest to you?

1. _____
2. _____
3. _____
4. _____
5. _____
6. _____
7. _____
8. _____
9. _____
10. _____

"My optimism wears heavy boots and is loud."

~ Henry Rollins

Describe one of your traits and in what ways it "is loud."

_____
_____

My Relationships with Intangible Things

Expanding Ideas to Contribute to My Character
Things I Would Not Want to Lose...

Create a poster, bumper sticker, or a tee shirt slogan to illustrate ...

Things I Would Not Want to Lose

TEENS – Relationships with People, Places and Things

Expanding Ideas to Contribute to My Character

FOR THE FACILITATOR

I. Purpose
To identify and expand ideas about intangible concepts that contribute to character.

II. General Comments
Plan a separate session for each page; present each page as suggested in *III a-c* below. Decide whether to use the Individual, Team or Board Activity Format and photocopy the appropriate number of handouts.

III. Possible Activities
a. Photocopy enough of the selected handouts for all individuals or teams, or a master copy for the board activity.
b. Write "intangible" on the board and ask its meaning (lacking material qualities, unable to be touched or seen by the senses yet can be felt by the heart and recognized by the mind).
c. Write the page title on the board and elicit few examples to verify that teens understand.

Examples for each page of *Expanding Ideas to Contribute to My Character*
- *I believe* … everyone deserves a chance; my best is good enough; in a Higher Power, etc.
- *Little Things That are Big* … a cruel whisper, a kind word, specific pet peeves, a *white lie*, etc.
- *Things That are Broken* within me … my dreams are shattered; a promise that was not kept, etc.
- *Things That are Broken* in my world … the ways people treat each other – stereotype, bully, etc.
- *Silent Things That are Loud* … a smile, a hug; a dirty look, unanswered text; turning away, etc.
- *Things I Would Not Want to Lose* … my health, a loved one, my values, goals, humor, etc.

Individual Format
- Distribute the selected page from among the *Expanding Ideas to Contribute to My Character* handouts.
- Allow time for completion; encourage teens to share responses and receive peer feedback.

Team Format
- Divide the group into teams; teams receive one handout and elect secretaries to write their ideas.
- Allow time for teams to complete the page; the group reconvenes.
- The secretaries share their teams' responses and receive feedback from other teams.

Board Activity
- Copy the handout onto the board.
- Encourage teens to brainstorm and take turns writing responses on the board.
- Alternatively a volunteer lists ideas on the board; teens give each other feedback.

For all formats
- Some pages have quotes and questions at the bottom of the page; be sure teens respond to these.

IV. Enrichment Activities
a. Encourage teens to identify intangible idea topics for a *Pass the Paper* project.
b. Teens write each idea as a heading at the top of a few papers.
c. The papers are circulated among the participants.
d. Each teen adds a response anonymously or signs their name.
e. The papers are then read aloud and discussed.

Intangible Idea Topic Possibilities
- Things That Money Can't Buy
- Positive Attributes
- What Is Success?
- What is Failure?
- Affirmations
- Random Acts of Kindness

My Relationships with Intangible Things

Rivalry Rhymes

I'm "Number One" Or I'm done.	Who won first place? May they fall on their face.	Friendly rivalry Brings out the best in me.	If I can't lead My heart will bleed.
Do my best Ignore the rest.	Teamwork: Share the blame Share the fame.	Working together Makes everyone better.	Win or lose Never snooze.
Supporting role Is not my goal.	If I don't score I'll play no more.	The greatest test? To applaud the best.	Winner: Pick up your pace There's another race.
Compared to you I think I'm through.	If I can congratulate I am giving up hate.	Social Network: Who has the most friends? The chase never ends.	Who's at the top? I hope they flop.

1. Write "Pro" in each box that suggests a positive aspect of competition or cooperation.
2. Write "Con" in each box that suggests a negative aspect of competition.
3. Write "Either" in each box that could refer to a positive or negative aspect of competition.
4. Draw a star in each box that sounds like something you would think.
5. Describe one of your experiences with competition.

_____

6. Describe one of your experiences with cooperation.

_____

7. Share a story about a time when you combined cooperation with competition.

_____

8. Write your own thoughts about competition and/or cooperation.

TEENS – Relationships with People, Places and Things

Rivalry Rhymes
FOR THE FACILITATOR

I. Purpose
To consider the pros and cons of competition and cooperation.

II. General Comments
Competition can motivate teens to do their best or devastate those who fear or feel, failure.

III. Possible Activities
   a. Write "Competition" on the board and ask its meaning (trying to win or do better than others).
   b. Write Cooperation" on the board and ask its meaning (working together to achieve a common goal).
   c. Encourage a brief discussion: Which is better – competition or cooperation? (individual opinions).
   d. Distribute the *Rivalry Rhymes* handout; volunteers take turns reading the rhymes aloud.
   e. Review the directions, numbers 1-8 with the group.
   f. Allow time for completion.
   g. Encourage teens to share their responses and reasons for numbers 1-3.

     Suggested Answer Key

Con	Con	Pro	Con
Pro	Pro	Pro	Either Pro or Con
Either Pro or Con	Con	Pro	Either Pro or Con
Con	Pro	Con	Con

     Rationale for "Either" responses:

- Win or lose, never snooze.
  Pro: keep working regardless of the outcome.
  Con: You get stressed by always needing to be the best
- Supporting role is not my goal.
  Pro: strive to be the star.
  Con: a supporting role is important whether at the Academy Awards, on a team, or in life.
- Winner: Pick up your pace, there's another race.
  Pro: Strive to beat your prior performances.
  Con: There's always another contest.

   h. Encourage teens to share their responses to numbers 4-8 and receive peer feedback.

IV. Enrichment Activities
Encourage individuals or teams to debate the pros and cons of competition in school, sports and work.

Possibilities

Place	Pros of Competition	Cons of Competition
School	Motivation to do one's best. Prepare for the real world challenges of competition. Learn to think and work independently.	Test scores become more important than learning. Cooperation is de-emphasized.
Sports	Teammates bond with one another as they face outside rivals. Players perform their best to stay on the team and help the team win.	Pressure to perform takes priority over family, friends, etc. Teammates may resent star players who get all the recognition.
Work	People push themselves out of their comfort zones. Incentives e.g. promotions and pay raises reward top performers. The organization benefits as people work harder.	Collaboration is inhibited. Comparing oneself to others can cause stress, misery, resentment, mistrust and envy.

My Relationships with Intangible Things ▶

Great Moments

"We are conditioned to think that our lives revolve around great moments. But great moments catch us unaware – beautifully wrapped in what others may consider a small one.

~ **Kent Nerburn**

Imagine pursuing great moments when small ones seem to interfere.

1. You are dressed in your best on your way to the prom. An elderly person has fallen on the sidewalk. What do you do?

2. You are hurrying to your team's big game when you see someone being bullied. What do you do?

3. You are studying for a final exam. Your younger sibling needs homework help. What do you do?

4. You are getting ready to go to a school play; an argument with your parent/caregiver sets you back. The adult drops a glass, which shatters into a million pieces.
What do you do?

5. You're walking to a movie with your partner when a homeless person asks for money for food. What do you do?

6. You're about to drive to your prospective college when your grandparents start talking about their alma maters. What do you do?

7. Complete this journal entry about something you have done or plan to do for someone. Your greatest moments may be known only to you – compassion for which you receive no credit.

Dear Diary, I feel really good about...

TEENS – Relationships with People, Places and Things

Great Moments

FOR THE FACILITATOR

I. Purpose
To recognize that small acts of kindness are big.

II. General Comments
When pursuing personal goals teens may ignore (or assist) people who need their time and attention.

III. Possible Activities
a. Write "Great Moments" on the board; ask teens to brainstorm examples (acing a test, graduation, getting one's driver's license, winning an award).
b. Distribute the *Great Moments* handout; a volunteer reads the quote and text above the questions aloud.
c. Allow time for completion.
d. Encourage teens to share their responses to numbers 1-6.
   Possibilities
   1. Stop; ask if you can call their family member or 911.
   2. Anonymously, call authorities for help.
   3. Help sibling with the homework for a specified period of time then resume studying.
   4. Help clean up the glass and then leave.
   5. Buy a take out meal or snack for the person.
   6. Listen with interest.
   7. Read the line above the box on the handout aloud:
      Explain that participants will not reveal their secret acts of kindness.
e. Ask about the value of *anonymous* compassionate acts (pure helpfulness with no personal glory).

IV. Enrichment Activities
a. Encourage teens to consider components of a Great Moments Campaign.
   Possibilities
   - Make posters promoting kindness.
   - Perform skits at school assemblies similar to the scenarios on the handout.
   - Write essays about *Small Moments That Are Big*.
   - Compose poems to describe *What Makes a Person Great?*
   - Create a *Catch Them in the Moment* movement – teens recognize peers who show kindness.
b. Encourage teens to start a *Great Moments Club*
   Possibilities
   - Members write their own name on slips of paper and place them in a container. They draw names and perform secret acts of kindness for the person whose name they picked.
   - Members support a worthwhile cause by raising funds for it. (car wash)
   - Members meet a need within their school (a canned or boxed food collection) from which students' families can anonymously obtain needed items.
   - Members volunteer at a food kitchen, clean up campaign, etc.
   - Members collect old eyeglasses, clothing, cell phones, etc., and donate them.
   - Members keep journals to record and reflect on their random acts of kindness.

My Relationships with Intangible Things

Ripples of Kindness

*"Remember there's no such thing as a small act of kindness.
Every act creates a ripple with no logical end."*

~ **Scott Adams**

Make your own ripples!

An act of kindness I have done in the past.

An act of kindness I would like to do now.

An act of kindness I would like to do as an adult.

What do you think the author of the quotation above means by *every act having no logical end?*

TEENS – Relationships with People, Places and Things

Ripples of Kindness
FOR THE FACILITATOR

I. Purpose
To illustrate the far-reaching effects of kindness.

II. General Comments
Teens will identify ways to show compassion and learn about unsought personal benefits.

III. Possible Activities
 a. Before session recruit a volunteer who will draw waves on the board when prompted.
 b. When session begins, ask the teen to draw today's topic on the board. (waves)
 c. Ask peers to guess what the volunteer drew.
 d. Write "Don't make waves" on the board and ask its meaning (don't upset people).
 e. Suggest that today teens will be making waves, by little ripples, one at a time, in a positive way.
 f. Distribute the *Ripples of Kindness* handout; a volunteer reads the quotation and directions aloud.
 g. Allow time for completion.
 h. Encourage teens to share their responses and receive peer feedback.
  Possibilities
   - Defend a person who is being bullied; speak out against cruelty.
   - Volunteer at a worthwhile organization.
   - Say something cheerful and/or thank people who work standing on their feet all day.
   - Eat lunch with someone new or a person that others exclude.
   - Return someone else's shopping cart.
   - Post uplifting notes for family members.
   - Make posters with positive slogans.
   - Give handwritten "I appreciate you ..." notes to family, friends, teachers and others.
   - Park further away from a store, restaurant etc.; leave closer spaces for those who need them.
   - Use interests and talents to help others, e.g., help a charity with electronics, sing at a hospital.
  Regarding the last question, what do you think the author of the poem above means by *every act having no logical end?* A person who receives kindness will usually treat others similarly; compassion may make all of the difference in the world; people who observe or hear about kindness are likely to help others.
 i. Reinforce that the best kind of kindness and compassion is expecting nothing in return. The self-satisfaction and knowledge that one has helped in some way is enough.
 j. Prompt teens to identify ways helping others also helps oneself (better physical and emotional health as teens focus on others rather than dwell on their own problems).

IV. Enrichment Activities
 a. Encourage teens to define *compassion* (a concern for others that motivates a desire to help).
 b. Write these proposed elements of compassion on the board.
  1. Notice how people are feeling.
  2. Feel empathy (put oneself in the person's situation and experience their feelings).
  3. Act to comfort, support and/or help them.
 c. Encourage individuals to write short stories that incorporate the three elements of compassion.
 d. Motivate teams to write scripts for mock videos that incorporate the three elements of compassion.
 e. Students read their short stories or perform mock videos and receive peer feedback.
 f. Ask teens to identify role models who show compassion (parents/caregivers, celebrities, etc.).
 g. Prompt teens to recognize ways they can become role models for younger family members, classmates, and others (encourage people to join them as they collect recyclables and donate the profits, help coach at the Special Olympics or a local team, shovel snow for elderly neighbors, etc.).

MY RELATIONSHIP WITH MYSELF 7

The most powerful relationship you will ever have is the relationship with yourself.
~ Steve Mariboli

Am I My Worst Enemy or Best Friend? .... page 115 ▶

Teens identify ways to support rather then sabotage themselves.
Teens practice talking to themselves as they would to a best friend regarding a current challenge.

My Feelings .... page 117 ▶

Teens realize that their thoughts, not persons or situations, affect their emotions.
Teens replace negative beliefs with more positive but realistic expectations.

In One Ear and… .... page 119 ▶

Teens filter messages to cast off destructive remarks and consider constructive criticism.
Teens link their self-concepts to comments they choose to ignore or believe.

The Power of Words .... page 121 ▶

Teens learn that their own words have the power to destroy or heal them.
Teens ponder words that protect them, promote their passion, uplift them and exemplify their positive traits.

Esteem-able .... page 123 ▶

Teens note admirable actions to promote self-esteem at home, school, work, with social media, etc.
Teens brainstorm ways to improve esteem through self-forgiveness and by rectifying wrongdoing.

Passwords for My Health .... page 125 ▶

Teens raise their awareness of mental and physical health habits by deciphering clues in a game.
Teens identify substances and activities to avoid.

What You See… .... page 127 ▶

Teens recognize how their mind's eye influences self-image and self-actualization.
Teens depict the actions they will take right now to become the person they want to be.

Are You Centered? .... page 129 ▶

Teens create a diagram that summarizes their ideas about self, others, places and things.
Teens identify balance regarding their bodies, minds and emotions.

My Relationship with Myself

Am I My Worst Enemy or Best Friend?

Traits of Me as My Own Worst Enemy

1. _____
2. _____
3. _____
4. _____
5. _____
6. _____
7. _____
8. _____

Traits of Me as My Own Best Friend

1. _____
2. _____
3. _____
4. _____
5. _____
6. _____
7. _____
8. _____

Sabotage or Support?

I am my own worst enemy when I ...

_____
_____
_____
_____
_____
_____

I am my own best friend when I ...

_____
_____
_____
_____
_____
_____

TEENS – Relationships with People, Places and Things

Am I My Worst Enemy or Best Friend?
FOR THE FACILITATOR

I. Purpose
To identify ways to support rather than sabotage self.

II. General Comments
Teens are encouraged to be their own best friend.

III. Possible Activities
a. Before session decide if teens will complete the top portion of the page in teams or individually.
   Team Option (recommended)
   - Before session photocopy the *Am I My Worst Enemy or Best Friend?* handout; cut on the broken lines; also cut down the middle of the Worst Enemy and Best Friend box.
   - The top will be done as teams; the Sabotage or Support questions will be answered individually.
   - Divide teens into two teams – *Friends* and *Enemies*; teammates sit together to confer.
   - Give the *Enemies* team the *Traits of Me as My Own Worst Enemy* section.
   - Give the *Friends* team the *Traits of Me as My Own Best Friend* section.
   - Prompt teens to ignore "me" and "my" and pretend they are talking about a made-up person (they can brainstorm without personal disclosure or claiming the traits at this time).
   - Each team elects a secretary to list their ideas.
   - Allow time for teams to list at least eight qualities.
   - The group re-convenes and secretaries read aloud their teams' lists.
     Possibilities

Traits of Me as My Own Worst Enemy	Traits of Me as My Own Best Friend
1. Judgmental	1. Non-judgmental
2. Put downs	2. Supportive
3. Self-deprecating	3. Speak well of myself
4. Unforgiveness	4. Forgive
5. Lie	5. Tell the truth
6. Diminish goals	6. Self-encouragement to meet goals
7. Accept with conditions	7. Accept unconditionally
8. Spread secrets	8. Keep confidentiality

b. After the team activity, distribute the bottom portion of the handout *Sabotage or Support?*
c. Teens will personalize their responses for this section (no longer using a fictitious person).
d. Allow time for individual completion.
e. Encourage teens to share their responses within their comfort zones and receive peer feedback.
   Examples
   - I am my own worst enemy when I... *put myself down, give up, endanger myself, etc.*
   - I am my own best friend when I... *use positive self-talk, persevere, promote my safety, etc.*
   Individual Option
   - Distribute the uncut *Worst Enemy or Best Friend?* handout to each teen.
   - Allow time for completion of the whole page; teens do not use a fictitious person.
   - Encourage teens to share responses within their comfort zones and receive peer feedback.

IV. Enrichment Activities
Encourage teens to take turns going to the front of the room and to talk to themselves, as they would to a best friend, regarding a current challenge they face.

My Relationship with Myself

My Feelings

Label the circles above with the feelings you experience most often.

Fill in the blank in the center circle.

TEENS – Relationships with People, Places and Things

FOR THE FACILITATOR

I. Purpose
To recognize that our personal thoughts affect emotions; no outside person or event can *make* us feel a certain way.

II. General Comments
Teens will replace some false beliefs with more realistic expectations.

III. Possible Activities
Before session decide whether to present the information as a board activity or individual exercise.

Board Option
- Draw a radial diagram similar to the one on the *My Feelings* handout on the board, but add more circles so each participant can label one.
- Encourage teens to take turns labeling the diagram with feelings they frequently experience.
- Allow teens to elaborate briefly about people and/or events associated with the feelings.
- Pose the question "Where do feelings come from"?
- List teens' responses in the center circle.
- Teens may think that people or events cause feelings; elicit that thoughts are primarily responsible.
- Explain that false beliefs can lead to sadness, anger, shame, jealousy, self-pity, etc.
- Ask "Why is it helpful to know that thoughts influence emotions?" (we can control our own way of thinking).

Individual Option
- Distribute the *My Feelings* handout and allow time for completion.
- Encourage teens to share responses; elicit that the center circle answer is *My feelings come from my thoughts*.

For either option continue as noted below

Write the following irrational ideas on the board and elicit realistic replacement thoughts.

Irrational thoughts to write on the board	Possible realistic replacement thoughts to elicit
That person made me upset.	*I upset myself.*
I need everyone's approval.	*I can't please everyone.*
Life should be fair.	*I can handle life's challenges.*
I must be perfect.	*I do my best.*
I am humiliated.	*I am human and humans make mistakes.*
Other (elicit ideas from teens)	
Other (elicit ideas from teens)	

IV. Enrichment Activity
a. Erase the examples that were written on the board.
b. Ask teens to anonymously write the thought(s) that cause them the most trouble on slips of paper.
c. Place the slips of paper face down in a container.
d. Teens take turns pulling a slip, reading the thought aloud and eliciting peer feedback regarding a more realistic replacement thought.
e. Facilitators may benefit from reviewing R.E.B.T (Rational Emotive Behavioral Therapy) and Cognitive Therapy to help teens further explore the effects of thoughts on feelings and actions.

My Relationship with Myself

In One Ear and...

In one ear...	Through my filter...	Then what?
		Out the other ear?
		To be considered?
		To internalize?

Messages about me that need to *go in one ear and out the other*:
_____
_____
_____

Constructive criticism to consider:
_____
_____
_____

Statements about me to *hear with both ears*:
_____
_____
_____

What my heart says about me that I want to internalize and believe:
_____
_____
_____

TEENS – Relationships with People, Places and Things

In One Ear and...
FOR THE FACILITATOR

I. Purpose
To cast off destructive criticism and consider constructive criticism; to implant positive messages.

II. General Comments
Teens' self-concepts depend partly on messages they choose to ignore or believe.

III. Possible Activities
   a. Before session procure a coffee filter (see "f" below); ideally have one filter per teen ("i" below).
   b. Ask what it means if something *goes in one ear and out the other* (it is ignored).
   c. Encourage teens to brainstorm examples (advice from someone they do not want advice from).
   d. Ask what it means to *listen with both ears* (pay close attention and hear what is being said).
   e. Encourage teens to brainstorm examples (information the teacher says will be on tomorrow's test).
   f. Display the coffee filter; ask its purpose (to allow flavor into the pot and keep out the grounds).
   g. Ask teens how minds can filter, in or out, what they hear (decide what to ignore and what to believe).
   h. Distribute the *In One Ear and...* handout; a volunteer reads the text in the boxes aloud.
   i. Coffee filters may be used instead of the handout; distribute one filter to each teen.
      Direct teens to divide their filters into four quarters and to do the following:
      - Write or depict each type of message on one quarter of the filter: *In one ear and out the other, constructive criticism, what to hear with both ears, what my heart says that I want to sink in.*
      - Scribble in examples of each type of message in each quarter (may use both sides of the filters).
   j. Allow time for completion.
   k. Encourage teens to share their responses and receive peer feedback.
      Examples
      - Messages to go in one ear and out the other:
         You're a loser.
         Why can't you be more like your brother?
      - Constructive criticism to consider:
         You need to study more.
         You need to be kinder to people.
      - Statements to hear with both ears:
         You can do it.
         You did your best.
      - What the heart says that needs to be internalized:
         I have a purpose.
         My ideas matter.

IV. Enrichment Activities
   a. Prompt teens to ponder the expression *Hear no evil.*
      Possibilities
      - Do not listen to damaging gossip.
      - Ignore listening to, or making, negative remarks about the school or workplace unless you can suggest solutions.
   b. Ask teens to identify when **to** hear evil, loudly and clearly.
      Examples
      - People who threaten to harm themselves, others or property.
      - Bullies who abuse potential victims.
   c. Emphasize the action required – tell a trusted adult or call 911 or their local emergency services.

My Relationship with Myself

The Power of Words

We define ourselves with our words.

Give an example of a word for each need:

- My shield   *(a word that protects me)*   _____
- My fire   *(a passion)*   _____
- My wing   *(something that uplifts me)*   _____
- My tool   *(a positive trait)*   _____
- My _____   _____
- My _____   _____

There exists for everyone a sentence – a series of words – that has the power to destroy you. Another sentence exists, another series of words, that could heal you.

~ Philip K. Dick

A sentence with the power to destroy me is ...
_____
_____

A sentence that could heal me is ...

TEENS – Relationships with People, Places and Things

The Power of Words

FOR THE FACILITATOR

I. Purpose
To understand to power of words to define and direct oneself.

II. General Comments
Teens may defeat themselves or promote possibilities with their words.

III. Possible Activities
   a. Write *The Power of Words* on the board.
   b. Ask teens why their own words are powerful (their words can help or harm themselves and others).
   c. Distribute *The Power of Words* handout.
   d. Allow time for completion.
   e. Encourage teens to share their responses and receive peer feedback.
   Possibilities
   - My Shield – *no, won't, don't, stop, boundaries, assertiveness, confidence, etc.*
   - My fire – *music, theater, art, poetry, altruism, sports, people, animals, etc.*
   - My wing – *spirituality, nature, higher power, family, faith, hope, etc.*
   - My tool – *compassion, education, cooperation, leadership, perseverance, honesty, etc.*
   - My _____ (teens may contemplate additional concepts).
   - A sentence with the power to destroy me is… *I'm ruined by my past; I can't, etc.*
   - A sentence with the power to heal is… *I am stronger because of my past; I can, etc.*
   f. Emphasize the strong tendency to believe the words we say aloud or to ourselves
   g. Encourage a discussion of words as weapons (put-downs, bullying, gossiping, lies, etc.).
   h. Ask teens to share times they had to *eat their words* or *took back* words they regretted saying.
   i. Promote the idea of different meaning of *eat my words*, that we consume what we say about ourselves and it becomes part of our self-concept.
   j. Ask teens to elaborate about times their words hurt or helped them.
   k. Encourage teens to brainstorm other types of destructive words – words that tempt teens to act against principles of health, safety and values.
   Possibilities
   - "It's cool to smoke."
   - "Just once it's ok to …" (text and drive, drink, have unprotected sex, etc.).
   - "Cheat on the test, everybody does it."

IV. Enrichment Activities
   a. Direct teens to do the following on the back of the handout:
   - Draw a locked box or chest.
   - Write a sentence that could destroy them in the box.
   - Draw the large outline of a key.
   - Write the sentence that could heal or save them on the key.
   b. Ask what they have illustrated.
   Elicit
   - Destructive words can be locked away until teens have the skills to defeat them.
   - Healing words are the key to remove and discard the negativity.
   c. Ask teens to consider the source of destructive messages (people who think they are giving good advice, those who want the teen to fail e.g. a jealous peer, and/or themselves through negative self-talk).

My Relationship with Myself

Esteem-able

A major way to positive self-esteem is to act *esteem-able*.

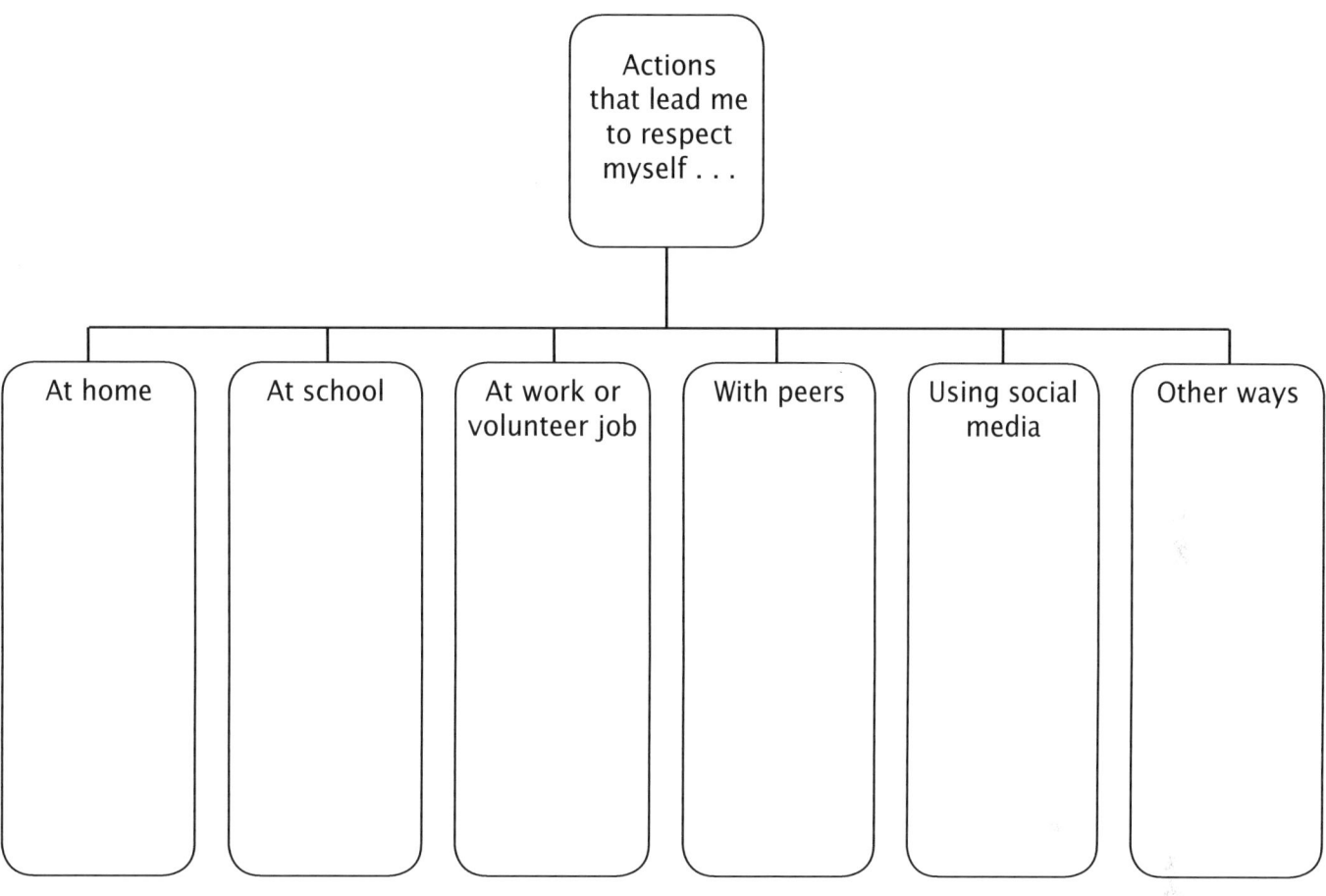

Actions that lead me to respect myself . . .

- At home
- At school
- At work or volunteer job
- With peers
- Using social media
- Other ways

Circle what you think is most important to elevate your self-esteem:

Positive thinking ▪ Praise from other people ▪ Your own actions

Explain:

_____
_____
_____
_____
_____
_____

TEENS – Relationships with People, Places and Things

Esteem-able
FOR THE FACILITATOR

I. Purpose
To reflect on positive actions to promote positive self-esteem.

II. General Comments
Teens' opinions of themselves can be based on admirable or negative actions.

III. Possible Activities
a. Write *Put your money where your mouth is* on the board and ask its meaning (do something rather than just talk about it).

b. Ask teens how their actions affect their opinions of themselves (contribute to positive or negative assessments).

c. Distribute the *Esteem-able* handout and ask teens to write at least one action in each category.

d. Allow time for completion.

e. Encourage teens to share their responses and receive peer feedback.

Possibilities
- Home – help with chores, treat family with respect, compromise.
- School – use study skills, help classmates, join activities, be a good sport.
- Work or volunteer job – be on time, accept supervision, cooperate with co-workers.
- Peers – include new, or people of different cultures than themselves, never bully, never gossip.
- Social media – text and post positive remarks, never write something you don't want the entire world to know.
- Others – help neighbors, join action organizations that better the world.

Elicit
- Positive thinking is strengthened when we reflect on our admirable actions.
- Praise from other people is nice but not always.
- Our actions, especially doing good when nobody sees, boost our own value in our own eyes.

IV. Enrichment Activities
a. Encourage teens to perform random acts of kindness, tell no one, but to privately journal about them.

b. Ask teens to brainstorm ways to improve low self-esteem related to wrongdoing.

Possibilities
- Acknowledge mistakes
- Decide to love oneself unconditionally despite disliking the behavior
- Make amends
- Apologize
- Right the wrong, if possible
- Learn from the experience
- Forgive self
- Prevent others from making the same errors, e.g. if you caused an accident by texting while driving, write an essay and read aloud to a class or submit to the school or local newspaper.

My Relationship with Myself ▶

Passwords for My Health

✂ -

Instructions for Game Show Host

- Explain to the group that the password game involves words related to physical and mental health.
- Point out that some words are helpful to health; others are things to avoid.
- Divide the group into pairs.
- Pairs of contestants take turns coming to the front of the room and facing each other.
- The pair decides who will give the clues and who will guess the password.
- The clue-giver pulls a cutout and gives one clue at a time to the guesser, without using any part of the word.
- Each clue may be one word only.
- A scorekeeper records each pair's points.
- Points:
  10 points if the word is guessed correctly after one clue.
  Nine points if the word is guessed correctly after the second clue.
  Eight points after the third clue, etc. through one point for guessing correctly after ten clues.
  If the word is not guessed after ten clues, zero points accrue and the word is revealed.
- The pair of contestants with the highest score wins.

✂ -

PASSWORDS

Vegetables	Nutrition	Sunscreen	Seatbelt	Exercise
Sleep	Floss	Brush	Breakfast	Protein
Water	Physician	Immunization	Acceptance	Helmet
Volume	Pedometer	Pets	Support	Wash
Text	Tobacco	Alcohol	Safety	Drugs
Sugar	Fats	Stress	Gratitude	No

TEENS – Relationships with People, Places and Things

Passwords for My Health
FOR THE FACILITATOR

I. Purpose
To identify habits to incorporate, and substances and activities to avoid.

II. General Comments
Teens play a game that raises their awareness of health-related concepts.

III. Possible Activities
 a. Before session photocopy the *Passwords for My Health* handout.
 b. Cut the words out and place them face down in front of the room.
 c. The Game Show Host reads the instructions; players give one word clues and guess the words.
  Ex: for *Floss*, clue-giver may say *teeth, string, dental, etc.*
 d. The game proceeds as stated on the handout's Game Show Host Instructions.

IV. Enrichment Activities
After the game, elicit concepts related to the passwords.

Possibilities
- Vegetables – high in vitamins and fiber
- Nutrition – choosing healthy foods in recommended daily amounts
- Sunscreen – helps prevent skin cancer
- Seatbelt – often saves lives and serious injuries
- Exercise – strengthens, energizes, improves mood
- Sleep – turn cell phone off at night to promote uninterrupted sleep
- Floss – important for dental and overall health
- Brush – practice the recommended technique and brush tongue also
- Breakfast – adequate protein and food fuels body and brain for the start of the day
- Protein – essential to the structure and function of living cells
- Water – drink plenty, replenish during exercise, when perspiring and /or ill
- Physician – regular physical check-ups and as questions or problems arise
- Immunization – recommended to prevent disease
- Acceptance – work with what cannot be changed
- Helmet – help prevents head injuries when biking, skating, motor cycling and sports
- Volume – too much damages ears - keep it down, especially in headphones
- Pedometer – activity tracker to signal the amount of movement
- Pets – promote physical exercise and provide unconditional love
- Support – positive encouraging relationships
- Wash –frequently to prevent disease
- Text – do not text and drive or walk, or while doing any activity that requires your complete attention
- Tobacco – avoid smoking and second-hand smoke; join a smoking cessation program if needed
- Alcohol – harmful to physical and mental health; causes accidents and deaths; seek help
- Safety – stick to rules of the road, rules for swimming and diving safety, information about safe sex or abstention, etc.
- Drugs – avoid street drugs and addictive prescription meds; seek help
- Sugar – limit sugary sodas and foods, and unsafe sweeteners; enjoy naturally sweet fruit
- Fats – avoid unhealthy fats; research sources of healthy fats
- Stress – learn coping skills to reduce distress to help mental and physical function
- Gratitude – thankfulness for your body, health, abilities, loved ones, etc. helps you feel better
- No – know your priorities and say *No* to time wasters, toxic people, unreasonable demands, etc.

My Relationship with Myself

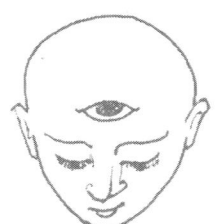

What You See...

Hold a picture of yourself long and steadily enough in your mind's eye, and you will be drawn toward it.
~ Napoleon Hill

What mental picture of yourself do you want to be "drawn to"?
Let your mind's eye guide you as you sketch, create cartoons or collages, use symbols and/or words to show what you will be doing and becoming.
Example: Practicing a sport to become a better player.

TEENS – Relationships with People, Places and Things

What You See...
FOR THE FACILITATOR

I. Purpose
To recognize that mental pictures influence self-image and actualization.

II. General Comments
Teens will employ visualization to motivate positive actions toward goals.

III. Possible Activities
  a. Write *What you see is ...* on the board; ask teens to finish the sentence; accept any responses.
  b. Add *...what you get* and ask teens to interpret the phrase, *what you see is what you get* (what you *see* or expect from others or yourself is usually what you get; can also mean "Take me as I am.")
  c. Recruit a volunteer to draw on the board.
  d. Whisper to the teen to draw an eye inside a brain.
  e. Encourage teens to decipher the illustration (what we visualize).
  f. Ask teens how their views of others can affect their behavior toward people.
  Possibilities
  - If they see someone they believe to be *unimportant*, they may ignore the person.
  - If they see someone they believe to be *popular*, they may pay attention to the person.
  g. Ask how their views of others can affect people's reactions to them.
  Possibilities
  - People they look down on may see them as mean.
  - People they see as worthwhile may see them as kind.
  h. Ask how their mind's eye influences who they become (positive or negative self-images can lead to productive or destructive actions).
  i. Distribute the *What You See ...* handout; a volunteer reads the quotation and directions aloud.
  j. Ask what is meant by *a picture of yourself* (what you are doing, not just physical appearance).
  k. Elicit that what teens mentally see themselves doing is often what they will actually do.
  l. Emphasize that teens' pictures need to show actions toward their goals because, as the quote says, they will be "drawn toward" what they visualize and depict.
  m. Allow time for completion.
  n. Encourage teens to share their work and receive feedback.
  Examples
  Teens may depict themselves becoming ...
  - Better students by studying
  - More outgoing by talking with peers
  - Generous by donating time or money to a charity
  - Compassionate by helping someone
  - Good athletes, musicians, etc. by practicing

IV. Enrichment Activities
  a. Motivate teens to share times their mental pictures resulted in positive and/or negative actions.
  b. Emphasize that visualization focuses on one's behavior, which can be controlled, not the outcome, which cannot be controlled (*Ex*: running one's best regardless of winning or losing the race).

My Relationship with Myself

Are You Centered?

At the center of your being you have the answer;
you know who you are and you know what you want.
~ Lao Tzu

Show with words, sketches and icons – your core, and people, places and things that keep you centered.

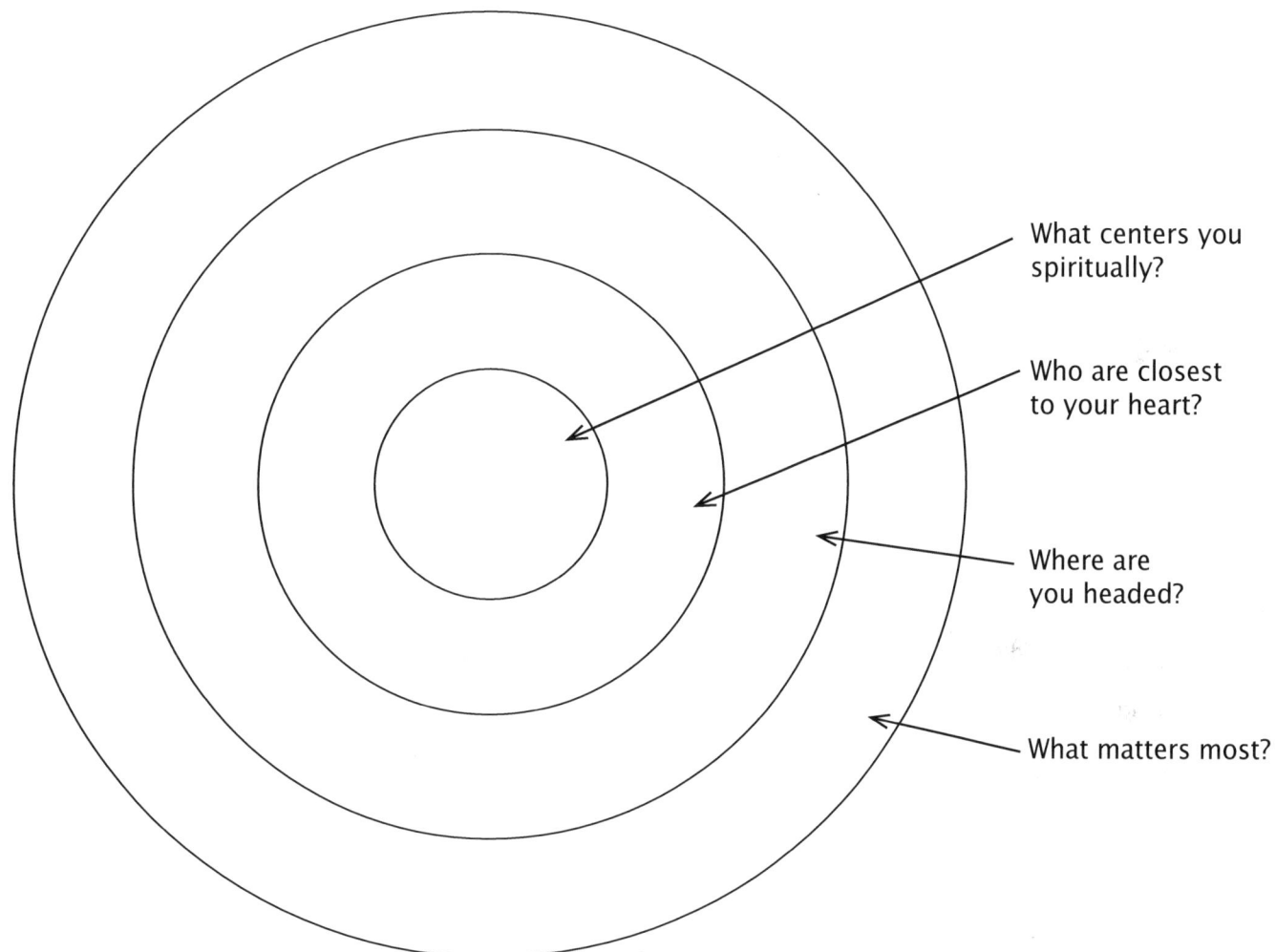

- What centers you spiritually?
- Who are closest to your heart?
- Where are you headed?
- What matters most?

How do you maintain your *balance* in ...

Your body?

_____

Your mind?

_____

Your feelings?

_____

TEENS – Relationships with People, Places and Things

Are You Centered?

FOR THE FACILITATOR

I. Purpose
To summarize ideas about self, others, places and things; to consider balance as an aspect of centeredness.

II. General Comments
Teens create a diagram of their relationships.

III. Possible Activities
a. Ask teens what it means to be "centered" (to know oneself, relate to others, adhere to values, etc.).
b. Remind teens that they have been exploring relationships and will now wrap-up their findings.
c. Distribute the *Are You Centered?* handout; a volunteer reads the quote, directions and questions aloud.
d. Allow time for completion.
e. Encourage teens to share their responses and receive peer feedback.

Possibilities
- Teens may be centered spiritually by
  Belief in a greater power; meditation, prayer; inspirational literature, music, art, nature.
- "Who...," "Where..." and "What..." relate to the people, places and things in teens' lives.
- Teens may maintain balance:
  Physically, through relaxation techniques, nutrition, exercise, satisfaction with one's body type.
  Intellectually, through curiosity, motivation for lifelong learning and pursuing a passion.
  Emotionally, through monitoring thoughts that affect feelings, expressing emotions by telling a trusted adult, sharing in group, using art, poetry, journaling, sculpting and other methods.

IV. Enrichment Activities
a. Suggest a Balance Bee:
  Teens brainstorm two-sided topics while standing.
  They sit when they run out of ideas.
  The last person standing can pose another question.

Possible Topics
- Ways to take care of yourself and ...
  Ways to care for others.
- Places that pose healthy risks and ...
  Places with potential dangers.
- Items worth saving money to buy and ...
  Causes worth spending money to help.
- Types of advice to tune in and ...
  Types of advice to tune out.
- When to follow a well-worn path ...
  When to make your own path.
- What battles are worth the (non-physical) fight?
  What is the "small stuff" not worth the sweat?

b. Encourage teens to think of their own Balance Bee Duos.
c. Compare centeredness to a wobbly toy that gets knocked down but bounces back upright.
d. Ask teens what helps them bounce back in tough times (spirituality, supportive people, learning from past trials what does and doesn't work, exploring options, hope that "this too shall pass").

WholePerson

Whole Person Associates is the leading publisher of training resources for professionals who empower people to create and maintain healthy lifestyles. Our creative resources will help you work effectively with your clients in the areas of stress management, wellness promotion, mental health and life skills.

Please visit us at our web site: **WholePerson.com.** You can check out our entire line of products, place an order, request our print catalog, and sign up for our monthly special notifications.

Whole Person Associates

800-247-6789